BRITISH WARSHIPS
& AUXILIARIES
1987/88 Edition

£3·00
STAR
7/31

Price
£3.95

THE ROYAL NAVY

"The General Council of British Shipping on behalf of British shipowners is delighted to hear of the protection being afforded to British merchant seamen and vessels operating in the Gulf area, by the presence of two Royal Naval warships.

"The GCBS is confident that this will enhance the safety of British trading ships.

"It was impressive that the Royal Navy Explosive Ordnance Disposal team arrived so quickly from the UK to render safe the missile that hit MV *Pawnee* on 23 September. The presence of HMS *Scylla* in Dubai provided some welcome reassurance for British owners and seafarers".

This statement, quoted in full, was issued by the GCBS last autumn and encapsulates what has for centuries been, and still remains, the Royal Navy's prime task: the protection of shipping upon which this country's economy and very survival still depend.

Britain is still a maritime nation relying upon world-wide trade, around 98 per cent of it carried by ships, regardless of what might be called "the Channel tunnel mentality" of those Little Englanders who see Britain today as no more than an off-shore appendage of Continental Europe with no significant part to play outside the European Economic Community.

Sea power is indivisible, according to the old maxim, and so long as we maintain an ocean-going Navy protection of merchant shipping vital to our survival cannot be solely a reflection of our commitments within NATO. Former Defence Secretary Sir John Nott, in a television interview last April, revealed the extent of his incomprehension of the meaning of sea power when he criticised the seven-month round-the-world deployment of an RN task group as being irrelevant to the Navy's paramount role of aiding Western defence of the Eastern Atlantic. In other words, it would seem, he and many others of like opinion would wish to serve notice that the Royal Navy would do its best to defy attempts to threaten our sea lifelines provided those threatening them would oblige by confining their activities to the Eastern Atlantic. What greater encouragement could there be for the Soviet Union or any other nation to look elsewhere outside the Atlantic for opportunities to threaten Free World shipping?

Britain no longer has the resources to be the world's policeman but should this mean abrogating any responsibilities beyond the 200 mile economic zone around our coasts and relegating the Navy to a coast guard role? In 1965 the then Labour Defence Secretary, Mr Dennis Healey, now the Party's Shadow Foreign Secretary, wrote in that year's Defence Estimates Statement: "Britain's defence policy has two purposes: to guarantee the nation's security and to contribute towards peace and stability in the world as a whole. These purposes are inseparable".

This summation of British defence policy is one that has been subscribed to by successive governments in the past 20 years and, without overseas bases, the task of contributing "towards peace and stability in the world as a whole" must today fall largely upon the Navy. Ships alone have the ability to provide a military presence without the political complications that can arise by having bases in somebody else's country or even from requests for over-flying rights for military aircraft through other nations' air space.

Yet there are those today who see the Navy's activities beyond the NATO area as detracting from its commitment to the Alliance even to the extent of suggesting that a ship deployed in the Gulf must be specially designed and therefore unsuitable to meet the NATO task. Absurd as such ideas are they illustrate the ignorance of many about the Navy in the 1980s which arises from a problem that the Service has always faced: ships overseas are out of sight to the public at home and therefore tend also to be out of the public mind.

But what purpose is served in deploying warships far beyond the NATO area in peacetime—a question that is even raised by some senior officers of the other two Services in the Ministry of Defence.

The General Council of British Shipping has already provided one answer but in the past year there have been many others.

In January the Royal Yacht *Britannia*, with a Russian officer on board as an adviser, was able to come close inshore to rescue hundreds of refugees of many nationalities caught in the cross-fire in the civil war in Aden. She was joined by the survey ship *Hydra* which had been carrying out a survey off Oman, the kind of task overseas still performed by the ships of the Hydrographer of the Navy that rarely receives public attention or recognition.

Thee months later in mid-April a task group left UK ports for a seven-month deployment that would take them around the world. A few hours after the carrier *Illustrious* the flagship of the group, labelled "Global '86", had sailed from Portsmouth a severe fire virtually destroyed one of her main gearboxes.

She returned to Portsmouth and, working round the clock, naval and civilian staff from the Fleet Maintenance and Repair Organisation completed the massive repairs 10 days early and the ship was able to sail to rejoin the rest of the "Global '86" ships at Singapore in mid-August. Sailors and dockyard staff worked side by side and the high degree of collaboration at all levels between all members of the base is something that "old Navy hands", with often some pretty strong views on "dockyard maties", find enormously heartening if not surprising. The idea of a naval artificer working on a lathe in a dockyard workshop aided by a civilian "matie", or vice versa, would have been almost unthinkable not so long ago.

But while *Illustrious* was being repaired the rest of the group, the Type 42 Sea Dart missile destroyer *Manchester*, the Seawolf missile armed frigate *Beaver*, the Type 21 frigate *Amazon*, the nuclear Fleet submarine *Swiftsure*, the Royal Fleet Auxiliary replenishment tankers *Olmeda* and *Bayleaf* and the RFA stores replenishment ship *Fort Grange* sailed westwards across the Atlantic. Because of restrictions imposed by many countries on visits by nuclear submarines the number of ports of call for *Swiftsure* was necessarily limited but, after time on the Falklands patrol, she was to play an important part in the five-nation Exercise RIMPAC in the central Pacific.

After visiting Caracas in Venezuela, the group's surface ships transited the Panama Canal and split up to visit San Diego and San Francisco in California and later Vancouver in Canada before starting RIMPAC in June.

The exercise involved two US carrier battle groups and ships from the Australian, Canadian and Japanese navies as well as the RN which was participating in a joint exercise in the Pacific for the first time since the early 1970s. The British ships were joined by RAF Nimrods operating from Pearl Harbour.

RIMPAC was clearly of enormous value for the RN and RFA ships, and lessons were learnt of great relevance even if the scenario were to be shifted to the Eastern Atlantic or elsewhere in the NATO area.

From Pearl Harbour the ships sailed to Pusan in S. Korea and *Manchester* and *Amazon* visited Shanghai, perhaps the highlight of "Global '86" and the first time RN ships had been in a Chinese port since 1980. The visit also underlined another important aspect of the RN's deployments overseas: assistance for Britain's trade. Among the many Chinese who toured the two ships was, unexpectedly, the Chief of Naval Staff (equivalent to the RN's First Sea Lord) Liu Huaqing, as well as

4

numerous heads of technical departments from the Defence Ministry in Peking. The result was that the many British companies who had sent representatives to Shanghai for the ships' visit found doors being opened to them, back in Peking, on which they had been knocking unsuccessfully for years in some instances.

But the Chinese interest was not confined to the ships' hardware. They were keen to learn about the internal organisation and administration on board; the responsibilities of various members of the ships' companies; how the RN disciplinary system works and a host of other topics concerning the way the Service "does its thing".

Now the chances are that the Chinese, who have already highly praised the instruction given them in a course on submarine tactics by the British Naval Attache (a submariner) in Peking, may seek further RN assistance when next year they re-establish the rank structure in their armed forces.

But there will be intense competition from other Western navies since they are well aware that training another nation's young officers today may well be sowing seeds for future purchases of equipment as these officers in years to come are in positions where they will influence the choice of equipment for their navies. Today the RN is training in Britain, or has overseas training teams and loan personnel instructing, officers and men of some 63 navies. This speaks volumes for the high regard many nations have for the service's professionalism.

From Shanghai and Hong Kong and ports in Malaysia the "Global '86" ships went on to visit ports in Australia, which included participation in the Royal Australian Navy's 75th birthday anniversary culminating in a review at Sydney by Prince Philip in early October. In late November the ships took part in exercise "Saif Sareea" off Oman, an exercise intended to test Britain's ability to make rapid reinforcement in troublespots beyond the NATO area. Men of 40 Commando Royal Marines landed in Oman from the assault ship *Intrepid*, the first time one of the RN's amphibious ships has been deployed East of Suez certainly since the early 1970s.

The visit of the frigate *Brazen* to Malta in August was another "first" for 10 years and she attracted 20,000 visitors, twice the number expected, with the locals displaying "welcome home" banners. Can the impact on ordinary people of such a visit really be equalled by the "diplomatic activity" which those who see no real task for the Navy today overseas would presumably substitute?

Such activities and many others of a more routine nature like the continuing presence of RN ships around the Falklands, at Hong Kong and in the West Indies and off Belize may serve to show that the RN still operates world-wide. Not only does this give experience in operating, often with other navies, in distant waters where port visits also undoubtedly foster British trade but it has an impact that, for an accountant, is unquantifiable and can best be called "goodwill". Then, too, there are sometimes purely humanitarian tasks such as disaster relief.

Yet there are some who see the cost of such tasks as detracting from the prime role of the RN in support of NATO and would for this reason drastically curtail or abolish them. If such a policy were to prevail it is perhaps not hard to see the likely impact on our trade, and thus on jobs; on our influence overseas and not least on the high regard (which also is a moneyspinner when translated into terms of training foreign navies) with which the RN is still held abroad. Money saved by such a policy would be minimal since, unless the ships were scrapped and their crews made redundant, maintenance, fuel and stores bills would still arise and crews would still have to be paid.

Under the present government there is recognition of the importance of the "out of (the NATO) area" role, as well as that of reinforcing NATO's northern flank in Norway, and this is demonstrated by the approval for the expenditure of £200 million on two new amphibious ships (which may be specially built or mercantile conversions). It is hoped there will also be a slightly longer term programme to modernise four of the RFA's Sir Lancelot class landing ships and to convert a container ship to carry comparable numbers of helicopters and Marines to those that once were embarked in the carrier *Hermes* before her sale to India in spring 1986.

The past year has seen the first salvos in what promises to be quite a battle in the next few years in new guns for the Navy. There are two schools: those who wish to see an adaptation of the Army's 155mm and those who support the Italian 127mm weapon which is the currently preferred option for the NATO Frigate Replacement (NFR 90) in which Britain along with seven NATO Allies is involved in feasibility studies.

Elsewhere in the weapons field, the year has seen the signing of a Memorandum of Understanding with the Americans for the joint development of the Advanced Sea Mine which in the 1990s could prove a potent weapon against submarines operating in Continental Shelf waters. The joint development programme is saving taxpayers £50 million in each country and further savings are likely in the production phase.

The new mines are part of a £1 billion 15 year programme, which began in 1980 and in which the RN is to get at least 13 Hunt class combined mine-hunters and 'sweepers; 16 River class minesweepers and, by 1995, the initial 10 of the new Sandown class of single-role minehunters. Equipment is also to be stockpiled for the rapid conversion of 30-40 offshore supply vessels into minesweepers, a task that would have fallen to our distant water trawler fleet but which now has dwindled to zero under the impact on traditional fishing grounds of other countries' 200 mile exclusive economic zones.

In early October the new survey ship *Roebuck* was formally commissioned and is arguably the most advanced ship of her type in the world with her new surveying sidescan sonar and SIPS—Survey Information Processing System—that will allow her to produce three-dimensional model plots of the seabed essential for the computerised navigational charts of the future.

The *Roebuck* replaced the ocean survey ship *Hydra*, which has been sold to Indonesia. Three more of the class were to have been built but appear to have been shelved indefinitely whilst *Hydra*'s sister ships *Hecate* and *Hecla* are now being paid off, five years ahead of the planned date.

The Hydrographer is far from alone in facing the problem of trying to make ends meet with dwindling resources. The annual ordering rate of three Type 23 frigates needed if 50 destroyers and frigates are to be retained in the operational fleet in the 1990s is slipping badly, and though three were ordered in the past year this cannot match the accelerating rate of paying off of older ships. The year has seen the paying off of the frigates *Yarmouth*, *Galatea* and *Leander*, the last two into the re-formed Standby Squadron and the first to be sunk as a target; the missile destroyer *Glamorgan* sold to Chile and two more Batch I Ikara anti-submarine missile armed Leanders due to pay off before the end of the year.

Though the Type 22 frigate *Brave*, the first to have Spey gas turbines giving her a range of 12,000 miles, was commissioned during the year and her sister ship *London* began contractor's sea trials the operational fleet is set to drop to 47 destroyers and frigates in 1987, since the partly disarmed destroyer *Fife* and frigate *Juno* in their permanent sea training roles can no longer be considered fully operational.

Similarly, the building rate of the Upholder class of diesel-electric submarines (SSK), with four currently under construction, will not match the decline in numbers of SSKs with *Sealion*, *Walrus*, *Oberon* and *Orpheus* already gone or soon to do so, leaving only 11 O class boats.

Though 1987 should see the completion of the Type 22 frigate *Sheffield* and possibly her sister ships *Cornwall* and *Coventry*, it should not be forgotten that all three are replacements for 1982 Falklands war losses and are not additions to the fleet.

Small wonder then that, only three months after completing a six month refit last April at Rosyth, it was felt some further three months' work repairing fire damage on board the 25 year old frigate *Plymouth* was worth the cost simply in

6

order to meet commitments. Now *Plymouth*, reprieved twice from the shipbreakers in 1981 and again in 1985, will sail on till 1988 along with her 26 year old sister ship *Rothesay*.

The reducing number of hulls may mean some shift towards at least a few more uniformed jobs ashore for, in the period April-December 1985, the number of men in all three Services quitting at their own request rose by almost 1,000 from 4,376 in the same period in 1984 to 5,366. For the Navy such figures are thought particularly to stress the "separation factor" from increasing time spent at sea. In the same periods the number of officers resigning at their own request rose from 879 to 999. The big increase in naval officer recruitment in the present financial year will do little to relieve the deliberately depressed recruiting in 1981-83 until the 1990s, when those joining now have passed through the training pipeline. Meanwhile the lack of manpower, with the 1981 "Nott cuts" still continuing to a total of 10,000 by 1991 (though in 1981 the cuts were to have been 10,000 by 1986 and a further 8,000 by 1991) is hitting the number of loan service and training staff that can be made available to other navies. A classic example of a false economy!

Besides the strain increased time serving in seagoing ships imposes on sailors' families and the men themselves, there are still a number of niggling factors in Service life whose removal would cost a tiny fraction of the waste that results when an experienced and highly trained man quits well before retirement date.

Most ships today refit at either Rosyth or Devonport but the encouragement of home-ownership in the Service in recent years means that many officers and ratings live outside Fife or Devon. But they must move at least 200 miles from their ship's homeport before they can qualify for "separation" travel warrants over and above the annual allocation. Men in ships refitting at Rosyth with homes in the Midlands, Tyne or Merseyside, for example, might, some maintain, just as well be serving off the Falklands or in the Gulf for all the extra time they get with their families.

At the root, of course, of almost all the problems facing the Service, whether it be new ships and equipment or travel warrants, is money. And the lack of that, it is being claimed in some quarters, is being increasingly compounded by the £10 billion or so cost of the Trident programme. The first of these submarines, *Vanguard*, was ordered last April and Vickers have now been invited to tender to build the second. The programme seriously began in 1980 when it was decided to opt for Trident to replace Polaris and the costs will be spread over some 18 years, something that critics tend to forget.

Such issues will no doubt be fully aired in the next year or so in the run-up to the general election. It is to be hoped, in all the welter of argument, sight is not lost of the Navy's continuing vital role in helping prevent the kind of situations arising in which the pro- or anti-nuclear arguments might be put to the real test.

7

SHIPS OF THE ROYAL NAVY — PENNANT NUMBERS

Ship	Penn. No.	Ship	Penn. No.
Aircraft Carriers		HERMIONE	F58
INVINCIBLE	R05	JUPITER	F60
ILLUSTRIOUS	R06	APOLLO	F70
ARK ROYAL	R07	SCYLLA	F71
HERMES	R12	ARIADNE	F72
		CHARYBDIS	F75
Destroyers		CAMPBELTOWN	F86
FIFE	D20	CHATHAM	F87
BRISTOL	D23	BROADSWORD	F88
BIRMINGHAM	D86	BATTLEAXE	F89
NEWCASTLE	D87	BRILLIANT	F90
GLASGOW	D88	BRAZEN	F91
EXETER	D89	BOXER	F92
SOUTHAMPTON	D90	BEAVER	F93
NOTTINGHAM	D91	BRAVE	F94
LIVERPOOL	D92	LONDON	F95
MANCHESTER	D95	SHEFFIELD	F96
GLOUCESTER	D96	COVENTRY	F98
EDINBURGH	D97	CORNWALL	F99
YORK	D98	ROTHESAY	F107
CARDIFF	D108	LEANDER	F109
		PLYMOUTH	F126
Frigates		PENELOPE	F127
AURORA	F10	AMAZON	F169
ACHILLES	F12	ACTIVE	F171
EURYALUS	F15	AMBUSCADE	F172
DIOMEDE	F16	ARROW	F173
GALATEA	F18	ALACRITY	F174
CLEOPATRA	F28	AVENGER	F185
ARETHUSA	F38		
NAIAD	F39	**Submarines**	
SIRIUS	F40	WALRUS	S08
PHOEBE	F42	ODIN	S10
MINERVA	F45	ORPHEUS	S11
DANAE	F47	OLYMPUS	S12
JUNO	F52	OSIRIS	S13
ARGONAUT	F56	ONSLAUGHT	S14
ANDROMEDA	F57	OTTER	S15

Ship	Penn. No.	Ship	Penn. No.
ORACLE	S16	CATTISTOCK	M31
OCELOT	S17	COTTESMORE	M32
OTUS	S18	BROCKLESBY	M33
OPOSSUM	S19	MIDDLETON	M34
OPPORTUNE	S20	DULVERTON	M35
ONYX	S21	BICESTER	M36
RESOLUTION	S22	CHIDDINGFOLD	M37
REPULSE	S23	ATHERSTONE	M38
RENOWN	S26	HURWORTH	M39
REVENGE	S27	BERKELEY	M40
UPHOLDER	S40	QUORN	M41
CHURCHILL	S46	BILDESTON	M1110
CONQUEROR	S48	BRERETON	M1113
COURAGEOUS	S50	BRINTON	M1114
TRENCHANT	S91	BRONINGTON	M1115
TALENT	S92	WILTON	M1116
TRIUMPH	S93	CRICHTON	M1124
VALIANT	S102	CUXTON	M1125
WARSPITE	S103	BOSSINGTON	M1133
SCEPTRE	S104	GAVINTON	M1140
SPARTAN	S105	HUBBERSTON	M1147
SPLENDID	S106	IVESTON	M1151
TRAFALGAR	S107	KEDLESTON	M1153
SOVEREIGN	S108	KELLINGTON	M1154
SUPERB	S109	KIRKLISTON	M1157
TURBULENT	S110	MAXTON	M1165
TIRELESS	S117	NURTON	M1166
TORBAY	S118	SHERATON	M1181
SWIFTSURE	S126	UPTON	M1187
		WALKERTON	M1188
Assault Ships		SOBERTON	M1200
FEARLESS	L10	STUBBINGTON	M1204
INTREPID	L11	WAVENEY	M2003
		CARRON	M2004
Minesweepers		DOVEY	M2005
& Minehunters		HELFORD	M2006
BRECON	M29	HUMBER	M2007
LEDBURY	M30	BLACKWATER	M2008

Ship	Penn. No.	Ship	Penn. No.
ITCHEN	M2009	STRIKER	P285
HELMSDALE	M2010	PUNCHER	P291
ORWELL	M2011	CHARGER	P292
RIBBLE	M2012	RANGER	P293
SPEY	M2013	TRUMPETER	P294
ARUN	M2014	JERSEY	P295
		GUERNSEY	P297
Patrol Craft		SHETLAND	P298
PEACOCK	P239	ORKNEY	P299
PLOVER	P240	LINDISFARNE	P300
STARLING	P241	**Minelayer**	
SWALLOW	P242	ABDIEL	N21
SWIFT	P243		
PROTECTOR	P244	**Survey Ships & RN**	
GUARDIAN	P245	**Manned Auxiliaries**	
SENTINEL	P246	BRITANNIA	A00
CORMORANT	P256	GLEANER	A86
HART	P257	MANLY	A92
LEEDS CASTLE	P258	MENTOR	A94
REDPOLE	P259	MILBROOK	A97
KINGFISHER	P260	MESSINA	A107
CYGNET	P261	ROEBUCK	A130
PETEREL	P262	HECLA	A133
SANDPIPER	P263	HECATE	A137
ARCHER	P264	HERALD	A138
DUMBARTON		ENDURANCE	A171
CASTLE	P265	WAKEFUL	A236
BITER	P270	ETTRICK	A274
SMITER	P272	ELSING	A277
PURSUER	P273	IRONBRIDGE	A311
ANGLESEY	P277	BULLDOG	A317
ALDERNEY	P278	IXWORTH	A318
BLAZER	P279	BEAGLE	A319
DASHER	P280	FOX	A320
ATTACKER	P281	FAWN	A335
CHASER	P282	CHALLENGER	K07
FENCER	P283		
HUNTER	P284		

This book is updated and re-issued every *December*. Keep up to date . . . Don't miss the new edition.

● HMS NEPTUNE

HMS Renown

RESOLUTION CLASS

Ship	Pennant Number	Completion Date	Builder
RESOLUTION	S22	1967	Vickers
REPULSE	S23	1968	Vickers
RENOWN	S26	1968	C. Laird
REVENGE	S27	1969	C. Laird

Displacement 8,400 tons (submerged) **Dimensions** 130m x 10m x 9m **Speed** 25 knots **Armament** 16 Polaris Missiles, 6 Torpedo Tubes **Complement** 147 (x 2).

Notes

These four nuclear-powered Polaris submarines are the United Kingdom's contribution to NATO's strategic nuclear deterrent. At least one of them is constantly on patrol and because of their high speed, long endurance underwater, and advanced sonar and electronic equipment they have little fear of detection.

Each submarine carries 16 Polaris two-stage ballistic missiles, powered by solid fuel rocket motors, 9.45 metres long, 1.37 metres diameter and weighing 12,700 kilogrammes with a range of 2,500 miles. The first of a new Vanguard Class has been ordered as eventual replacements for this class.

HMS Conqueror

VALIANT CLASS

Ship	Pennant Number	Completion Date	Builder
CHURCHILL	S46	1970	Vickers
CONQUEROR	S48	1971	C. Laird
COURAGEOUS	S50	1971	Vickers
VALIANT	S102	1966	Vickers
WARSPITE	S103	1967	Vickers

Displacement 4,900 tons dived **Dimensions** 87m x 10m x 8m **Speed** 28 knots + **Armament** 6 Torpedo Tubes **Complement** 103.

Notes
DREADNOUGHT—the forerunner of this class—is awaiting disposal (by scrap or sinking) at Rosyth. These boats are capable of high underwater speeds and can remain on patrol almost indefinitely. They are able to circumnavigate the world without surfacing.

• HMS NEPTUNE

HMS Sceptre

SWIFTSURE CLASS

Ship	Pennant Number	Completion Date	Builder
SCEPTRE	S104	1978	Vickers
SPARTAN	S105	1979	Vickers
SPLENDID	S106	1980	Vickers
SOVEREIGN	S108	i974	Vickers
SUPERB	S109	1976	Vickers
SWIFTSURE	S126	1973	Vickers

Displacement 4,500 tons dived **Dimensions** 83m x 10m x 8m **Speed** 30 knots + dived **Armament** 5 Torpedo Tubes **Complement** 116.

Notes
A follow-on class of ships from the successful Valiant Class. These submarines have an updated Sonar and Torpedo system. All are based at Devonport.

13

HMS Trafalgar

TRAFALGAR CLASS

Ship	Pennant Number	Completion Date	Builder
TRENCHANT	S91	1987	Vickers
TRAFALGAR	S107	1983	Vickers
TURBULENT	S110	1984	Vickers
TIRELESS	S117	1985	Vickers
TORBAY	S118	1986	Vickers
TALENT	S92	Building	Vickers
TRIUMPH	S93	Building	Vickers

Displacement 4,500 tons **Dimensions** 85m x 10m x 8m **Speed** 30 + dived **Armament** 5 Torpedo Tubes **Complement** 97.

Notes
Designed to be considerably quieter than previous submarines. Hull is covered with noise reducing tiles. These boats also have a greater endurance & speed than their predecessors.

14

● HMS NEPTUNE

HMS Walrus

PORPOISE CLASS

Ship	Pennant Number	Completion Date	Builder
WALRUS	S08	1961	Scotts *DELETE*

Displacement 2,410 tons (submerged) **Dimensions** 90m x 8m x 5m **Speed** 12 knots surfaced, 17 submerged **Armament** 8 Torpedo Tubes **Complement** 70.

Notes
Sole survivor of the Porpoise class of diesel powered submarines—the first to be designed and built after the war. Capable of long under-water patrols, but mainly used for exercise and training purposes as more Nuclear submarines join the Fleet. By late 1986 an order for four conventional submarines (to be named UPHOLDER, UNSEEN, URSULA, and UNICORN) had been placed. An eventual building rate of 1 per year is expected. Sealion paid off for scrap at the end of 1986. Walrus will follow in late 1987.   *HUNTBER SHIP BREAKERS.*

15

OBERON CLASS

HMS Odin

Ship	Pennant Number	Completion Date	Builder
ODIN	S10	1962	C. Laird
ORPHEUS	S11	1960	Vickers
OLYMPUS	S12	1962	Vickers
OSIRIS	S13	1964	Vickers
ONSLAUGHT	S14	1962	Chatham D'yard
OTTER	S15	1962	Scotts
ORACLE	S16	1963	C. Laird
OCELOT	S17	1964	Chatham D'yard
OTUS	S18	1963	Scotts
OPOSSUM	S19	1964	C. Laird
OPPORTUNE	S20	1964	Scotts
ONYX	S21	1967	C. Laird

Displacement 2,410 tons (submerged) **Dimensions** 90m x 8m x 5m **Speed** 12 knots surface, 17 knots submerged **Armament** 8 Torpedo Tubes **Complement** 70.

Notes
OPOSSUM and OTTER are fitted with new bow sonars—others will follow. OBERON paid off for scrap December 1986. ORPHEUS will be reduced to a static training vessel in mid 1987.

HUMBER

● HMS ILLUSTRIOUS

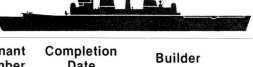

HMS Illustrious

INVINCIBLE CLASS

Ship	Pennant Number	Completion Date	Builder
INVINCIBLE	R05	1979	Vickers
ILLUSTRIOUS	R06	1982	Swan-Hunter
ARK ROYAL	R07	1985	Swan-Hunter

Displacement 19,500 tons **Dimensions** 206m x 32m x 6.5m **Speed** 28 knots **Armament** Sea Dart Missile, 2 x 20mm guns, 2 Phalanx **Aircraft** 5 x Sea Harrier, 10 x Sea King **Complement** 900 + aircrews.

Notes
Eventually eight Sea Harriers will be embarked in each ship—but one ship will always be in refit/reserve. INVINCIBLE is currently in long refit at Devonport. Armament alterations can be expected from those listed above.

17

AIRCRAFT CARRIERS

AUTHOR'S PHOTO   **HMS Hermes**

HERMES CLASS

Ship	Pennant Number	Completion Date	Builder
HERMES	R12	1959	Vickers

Displacement 28,700 tons **Dimensions** 229m x 27m x 9m **Speed** 28 knots **Armament** 2 Sea Cat Missile Systems, 9 Sea King helicopters, 5 Sea Harrier aircraft, 2 Wessex helicopters **Complement** 980 + aircrews.

Notes
A former fixed wing aircraft carrier converted to a Commando Carrier in 1971-73. Refitted in 1976 into an anti-submarine Carrier and again in 1981 (for Sea Harrier operations). Flagship for the Falkland Islands Task Force. Refitted at Devonport during 1986 for transfer to Indian Navy in Early 1987.

M. LENNON

FEARLESS CLASS

HMS Intrepid

Ship	Pennant Number	Completion Date	Builder
FEARLESS	L10	1965	Harland & Wolff
INTREPID	L11	1967	J. Brown

Displacement 12,500 tons, 19,500 tons(flooded) **Dimensions** 158m x 24m x 8m **Speed** 20 knots **Armament** 2 Sea Cat Missile Systems, 2 x 40mm guns, 2 x 30mm + 2 x 20mm (INTREPID only). **Complement** 580.

Notes
Multi-purpose ships that can operate helicopters for embarked Royal Marine Commandos. 4 landing craft are carried on an internal deck and are flooded out when ship docks down. One ship is usually in refit/reserve (currently FEARLESS). Long term future of both ships under discussion.

19

W. SARTORI

BRISTOL CLASS (Type 82)

HMS Bristol

Ship	Pennant Number	Completion Date	Builder
BRISTOL	D23	1972	Swan Hunter

Displacement 6,750 tons **Dimensions** 154m x 17m x 7m **Speed** 30 knots + **Armament** 1 x 4.5″ gun, 1 Sea Dart Missile System, 4 x 30mm + 4 x 20mm guns **Complement** 407.

Notes
Four ships of this class were ordered but three later cancelled when requirement for large escorts for fixed wing aircraft carriers ceased to exist. Helicopter Deck provided but no aircraft normally carried. Fitted for, but not with, Vulcan Phalanx. Frequently employed as a Flagship.

HMS Fife

COUNTY CLASS

Ship	Pennant Number	Completion Date	Builder	
				CHILÉ
FIFE	D20	1966	Fairfield	●

Displacement 6,200 tons **Dimensions** 159m x 16m x 6m **Speed** 32 knots **Armament** 2 x 4.5″ guns, 2 x 20mm guns, 4 x 30mm guns, 4 Exocet Missiles, 2 x Seacat. Torpedo Tubes **Complement** 485.

Notes
Employed as a training ship for young officers from BRNC Dartmouth. Sea Slug missile system removed and classrooms added. GLAMORGAN sold to Chile 1986.

21

HMS Gloucester

SHEFFIELD CLASS (Type 42)

Ship	Pennant Number	Completion Date	Builder
BIRMINGHAM	D86	1976	C. Laird
NEWCASTLE	D87	1978	Swan Hunter
GLASGOW	D88	1978	Swan Hunter
EXETER	D89	1980	Swan Hunter
SOUTHAMPTON	D90	1981	Vosper T.
NOTTINGHAM	D91	1982	Vosper T.
LIVERPOOL	D92	1982	C. Laird
● MANCHESTER	D95	1983	Vickers
● GLOUCESTER	D96	1984	Vosper T.
● EDINBURGH	D97	1985	C. Laird
● YORK	D98	1984	Swan Hunter
CARDIFF	D108	1979	Vickers

Displacement 3,660 tons **Dimensions** 125m x 15m x 7m **Speed** 30 knots + **Armament** 1 x 4.5″ gun, 4 x 30mm guns, 4 x 20mm guns, Sea Dart Missile System: Lynx Helicopter. 6 Torpedo Tubes **Complement** 280 + ● "stretched" Type 42.

Notes
● "Stretched" versions are 14 metres longer than earlier vessels of the class.

22

● S. KENT

HMS Battleaxe

BROADSWORD
CLASS (Type 22) (Batch 1)

Ship	Pennant Number	Completion Date	Builder
BROADSWORD	F88	1978	Yarrow
BATTLEAXE	F89	1980	Yarrow
BRILLIANT	F90	1981	Yarrow
BRAZEN	F91	1982	Yarrow

Displacement 3,860 tons **Dimensions** 131m x 15m x 6m **Speed** 29 knots **Armament** 4 Exocet Missiles, 2 Sea Wolf Missile Systems, 2 x 40mm guns, 2 or 4 x 20mm guns, 6 Torpedo Tubes, 2 Lynx Helicopters **Complement** 224.

Notes
Planned successor to the Leander Class. Although capable of carrying 2 helicopters, normally only 1 embarked.

23

F
R
I
G
A
T
E
S

HMS Brave

BROADSWORD CLASS (TYPE 22) (BATCH 2 & 3)

Ship	Pennant Number	Completion Date	Builder
CAMPBELTOWN	F86	Building	C. Laird
CHATHAM	F87	Building	Swan Hunter
● BOXER	F92	1983	Yarrow
● BEAVER	F93	1984	Yarrow
● BRAVE	F94	1985	Yarrow
● LONDON	F95	1986	Yarrow
● SHEFFIELD	F96	1987	Swan Hunter
● COVENTRY	F98	Building	Swan Hunter
CORNWALL	F99	1987	Yarrow

Displacement 4100 tons **Dimensions** 143m x 15m x 6m **Speed** 30 knots **Armament** 4 Exocet Missiles, 2 Sea Wolf Missile Systems, 2 x 40mm + 2 x 20mm guns, 6 Torpedo Tubes, 2 Lynx Helicopters **Complement** 290 ● are Batch 2 ships.

24

HMS Achilles

LEANDER CLASS

Ship	Pennant Number	Completion Date	Builder
ACHILLES	F12	1970	Yarrow
DIOMEDE	F16	1971	Yarrow
JUNO	F52	1967	Thornycroft
APOLLO	F70	1972	Yarrow
ARIADNE	F72	1972	Yarrow

Displacement 2,962 tons **Dimensions** 113m x 13m x 5m **Speed** 27 knots **Armament** 2 x 4.5″ guns, 3 x 20mm guns, 1 Sea Cat Missile system, 1 Mortar Mk10, 1 Wasp helicopter **Complement** 260.

Notes
JUNO (with a much reduced armament) is a training ship. Most were due to be paid off into reserve but have been refitted for further service in the active fleet.

The first of a new Duke Class (Type 23) have been ordered and will be named HMS NORFOLK, ARGYLL, LANCASTER and MARLBOROUGH.

HMS Aurora

LEANDER CLASS (Ikara Conversions)

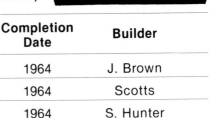

Ship	Pennant Number	Completion Date	Builder
AURORA	F10	1964	J. Brown
EURYALUS	F15	1964	Scotts
GALATEA ●	F18	1964	S. Hunter
ARETHUSA	F38	1965	Whites
NAIAD	F39	1965	Yarrow
LEANDER ●	F109	1963	Harland & Wolff

Displacement 2,860 tons **Dimensions** 113m x 12m x 5m **Speed** 29 knots **Armament** 1 Ikara Anti-submarine Missile, 2 x 40mm guns, 2 Sea Cat Missile Systems, 1 Mortar Mk10, 1 Wasp helicopter **Complement** 240.

Notes
All ships were converted (1973-76) to carry the Ikara Anti-submarine Missile System (forward of the bridge) in lieu of a 4.5″ gun. All are expected to be deleted from the active fleet within the next 2-3 years except ARETHUSA which is fitted with Towed Array Sonar. ● Ships in Reserve at Portsmouth.

● P.J. PACKENAS

HMS Andromeda

LEANDER CLASS
(Sea Wolf Conversions)

Ship	Pennant Number	Completion Date	Builder
ANDROMEDA	F57	1968	HM Dockyard Portsmouth
HERMIONE	F58	1969	Stephen
JUPITER	F60	1969	Yarrow
SCYLLA	F71	1970	HM Dockyard Devonport
CHARYBDIS	F75	1969	Harland & Wolff

Displacement 2,962 tons **Dimensions** 113m x 13m x 5m **Speed** 27 knots **Armament** Sea Wolf System, 4 x Exocet Missiles, 2 x 40mm guns, 1 Lynx helicopter **Complement** 260.

Notes
The refitting of these ships has cost in the region of £70m—ten times their original cost—but they are now packed with the latest anti-submarine technology. All Leander Class have small armaments, which vary between individual ships.

● P.J. PACKENAS

HMS Argonaut

LEANDER CLASS (Exocet Conversions)

Ship	Pennant Number	Completion Date	Builder
● CLEOPATRA	F28	1966	HM Dockyard Devonport
● SIRIUS	F40	1966	HM Dockyard Portsmouth
● PHOEBE	F42	1966	Stephens
MINERVA	F45	1966	Vickers
DANAE	F47	1967	HM Dockyard Devonport
● ARGONAUT	F56	1967	Hawthorn Leslie
PENELOPE	F127	1963	Vickers

Displacement 2,860 tons **Dimensions** 113m x 12m x 5m **Speed** 27 knots **Armament** 4 Exocet Missiles, 3 Sea Cat Missile Systems, 2 x 40mm guns, 6 Torpedo Tubes, 1 Lynx helicopter **Complement** 230.

Notes
The highly successful Leander Class are the last steam powered frigates in the Royal Navy, all later ships being propelled by gas turbines. ● ships have been refitted with the latest Towed Array sonar and their armament has been reduced to 2 Sea Cat systems and the 40mm guns replaced by 20mm weapons.

28

HMS Active

AMAZON CLASS (Type 21)

Ship	Pennant Number	Completion Date	Builder
AMAZON	F169	1974	Vosper T.
ACTIVE	F171	1977	Vosper T.
AMBUSCADE	F172	1975	Yarrow
ARROW	F173	1976	Yarrow
ALACRITY	F174	1977	Yarrow
AVENGER	F185	1978	Yarrow

Displacement 3,250 tons **Dimensions** 117m x 13m x 6m **Speed** 30 knots **Armament** 1 x 4.5″ gun, 2 x 20mm guns, 4 Exocet Missiles, 1 Sea Cat Missile System, 1 Lynx helicopter, 6 Torpedo Tubes **Complement** 170.

Notes
These General Purpose frigates were built to a commercial design by Vosper/ Yarrow and subsequently sold to the Ministry of Defence. All of the class have been given extra hull strengthening (see photo).

29

HMS Rothesay

ROTHESAY CLASS (Type 12)

Ship	Pennant Number	Completion Date	Builder
ROTHESAY	F107	1960	Yarrow
PLYMOUTH	F126	1961	HM Dockyard Devonport

Displacement 2,800 tons **Dimensions** 113m x 13m x 5m **Speed** 30 knots **Armament** 2 x 4.5″ guns, up to 4 x 20mm guns, 1 Sea Cat Missile System, 1 Mortar Mk10, 1 Wasp helicopter **Complement** 250.

Notes
Sole survivors of the successful Type 12 Class. The Leander Class were developed from this class. PLYMOUTH repaired for further service after major fire in 1986.

HMS Cottesmore

MINE COUNTERMEASURES SHIPS (MCMV'S)
BRECON CLASS

Ship	Completion Date	Pennant Number	Builder
BRECON	1980	M29	Vosper T.
LEDBURY	1981	M30	Vosper T.
CATTISTOCK	1982	M31	Vosper T.
COTTESMORE	1983	M32	Yarrow
BROCKLESBY	1983	M33	Vosper T.
MIDDLETON	1984	M34	Yarrow
DULVERTON	1983	M35	Vosper T.
BICESTER	1986	M36	Vosper T.
CHIDDINGFOLD	1984	M37	Vosper T.
ATHERSTONE	1987	M38	Vosper T.
HURWORTH	1985	M39	Vosper T.
BERKELEY	Building	M40	Vosper T.
QUORN	Building	M41	Vosper T.

Displacement 625 tonnes **Dimensions** 60m x 10m x 2.2m **Speed** 17 knots **Armament** 1 x 40mm gun **Complement** 45.

Notes

The largest warships ever built of glass reinforced plastic. Designed to replace the Coniston Class—their cost (£35m) has dictated the size of the class. Very sophisticated ships—and lively seaboats! A new vessel—the Single Role Minehunter (to be named HMS SANDOWN) has been ordered for 1989 delivery.

HMS Brereton

CONISTON CLASS

Ship	Penn. No.	Ship		Penn. No.
BILDESTON (H)	M1110	KIRKLISTON (H)	●	M1157
BRERETON (H)	M1113	MAXTON (H)		M1165
BRINTON (H)	M1114	NURTON (H)		M1166
BRONINGTON (H)	M1115	SHERATON (H)		M1181
WILTON (H)	M1116	§UPTON (S)		M1187
CUXTON (S)	M1125	WALKERTON (S)	●	M1188
BOSSINGTON (H)	M1133	§SOBERTON (S)		M1200
GAVINTON (H)	M1140	STUBBINGTON (S)	●	M1204
HUBBERSTON (H)	M1147			
IVESTON (H)	M1151			
KEDLESTON (H)	M1153	● In Reserve at		
KELLINGTON (H)	M1154	Portsmouth		

● K GIBSON

HMS Bronington

CONISTON CLASS (Cont.)

Displacement 425 tons **Dimensions** 46m x 9m x 3m **Speed** 15 knots **Armament** 1 x 40mm gun, 2 x 20mm guns (removed in some ships) **Complement** 29/38.

Notes

120 of this class were built in the early 50s but most have now been sold overseas or scrapped. They have fulfilled many roles over the years and have given excellent service. WILTON, built of glassfibre in 1973, was the world's first 'plastic' warship. Ships marked § are employed on Coastal Fishery Protection duties. Ships marked (S) are Minesweepers—(H) Minehunters.

● M LOUAGIE

HMS Itchen

FLEET MINESWEEPERS
RIVER CLASS

Ship	Pennant Number	Completion Date	Builder
WAVENEY	M2003	1984	Richards
CARRON	M2004	1984	Richards
DOVEY	M2005	1984	Richards
HELFORD	M2006	1984	Richards
HUMBER	M2007	1985	Richards
BLACKWATER	M2008	1985	Richards
ITCHEN	M2009	1985	Richards
HELMSDALE	M2010	1985	Richards
ORWELL	M2011	1985	Richards
RIBBLE	M2012	1985	Richards
SPEY	M2013	1985	Richards
ARUN	M2014	1986	Richards

Displacement 850 tons **Dimensions** 47m x 10m x 3m **Speed** 14 knots **Armament** 1 x 40mm, 2 x GPMG **Complement** 30.

Notes

Built as replacements for the MCM ships serving with the RNR. BLACKWATER has an RN ships company and is now in the Fishery Protection Squadron (FPS). Built to commercial specifications with steel hulls. Designed for 'sweeping in deep water. An order for four more of this class can be expected shortly to replace ships in the FPS.

34

M. LENNON

HMS Abdiel

**MINELAYER
ABDIEL CLASS**

Ship	Pennant Number	Completion Date	Builder
ABDIEL	N21	1967	Thornycroft

Displacement 1,500 tons **Dimensions** 80m x 13m x 4m **Speed** 16 knots **Armament** 44 mines. 1 x 40mm gun**Complement** 77.

Notes
Designed as a Headquarters and Support Ship for mine counter measure forces and exercise minelayer. Workshops & spares embarked enable minecountermeasures ships to operate well away from home bases.
ABDIEL is the only operational minelayer in the Royal Navy but plans exist to use merchant ships to lay mines if required. Due to be paid off, without replacement, within 2 years.

HMS Leeds Castle

CASTLE CLASS

Ship	Pennant Number	Completion Date	Builder
LEEDS CASTLE	P258	1981	Hall Russell
DUMBARTON CASTLE ●	P265	1982	Hall Russell

Displacement 1,450 tons **Dimensions** 81m x 11m x 3m **Speed** 20 knots **Armament** 1 x 40mm gun **Complement** 40.

Notes
These ships have a dual role—that of fishery protection and off-shore patrols within the limits of UK territorial waters. Unlike the Island Class these ships are able to operate helicopters—including Sea King aircraft. Trials have been conducted to assess the suitability of these ships as Minelayers. The 40mm gun could be replaced by the Oto Melara 76mm if required.

● Now in service as a Falkland Island Patrol vessel.

36

● P.W. BALL

ISLAND CLASS

Ship	Pennant Number	Completion Date	Builder
ANGLESEY	P277	1979	Hall Russell
ALDERNEY	P278	1979	Hall Russell
JERSEY	P295	1976	Hall Russell
GUERNSEY	P297	1977	Hall Russell
SHETLAND	P298	1977	Hall Russell
ORKNEY	P299	1977	Hall Russell
LINDISFARNE	P300	1978	Hall Russell

Displacement 1,250 tons **Dimensions** 60m x 11m x 4m **Speed** 17 knots **Armament** 1 x 40mm gun **Complement** 39.

Notes
Built on trawler lines these ships were introduced to protect the extensive British interests in North Sea oil installations and to patrol the 200 mile fishery limit.

37

PATROL VESSELS

HMS Swift

PEACOCK CLASS

Ship	Pennant Number	Completion Date	Builder
PEACOCK	P239	1983	Hall Russell
PLOVER	P240	1983	Hall Russell
STARLING	P241	1984	Hall Russell
SWALLOW	P242	1984	Hall Russell
SWIFT	P243	1984	Hall Russell

Displacement 700 tons **Dimensions** 60m x 10m x 5m **Speed** 28 knots **Armament** 1 x 76mm gun **Complement** 31.

Notes
The first warships to carry the 76mm Oto Melara gun. They are used to provide an ocean going back-up to the Marine Department of the Hong Kong Police. The Government of Hong Kong has paid 75% of the building and maintenance costs of these vessels.

38

 **HMS Protector**

Ship	Pennant Number	Completion Date	Builder	
PROTECTOR	P244	1975	Drypool Selby	✳
GUARDIAN	P245	1975	Beverley	✳
SENTINEL	P246	1975	Husumwerft	

Displacement 802 tons **Speed** 14 knots **Armament** 2 x 40mm **Complement** 24/6.

Notes

Formerly Oil Rig support vessels Seaforth Saga, Seaforth Champion and Seaforth Warrior (respectively) purchased from Seaforth Maritime Ltd. They are permanent Falkland Island Patrol Vessels—but their future in the South Atlantic is uncertain. SENTINEL is larger than the other two ships.

M. LOUAGIE   **HMS Biter**

COASTAL TRAINING CRAFT
ARCHER CLASS

Displacement 43 tonnes **Dimensions** 20m x 6m x 1m **Speed** 20 knots **Armament** Nil **Complement** 14

Ship	Pennant Number	Completion Date	Builder
ARCHER	P264	1985	Watercraft
BITER	P270	1985	Watercraft
SMITER	P272	1986	Watercraft
PURSUER	P273		
BLAZER	P279	**Ship**	**Pennant Number**
DASHER	P280		
PUNCHER	P291	RANGER	P293
CHARGER	P292	TRUMPETER	P294

Notes
For service with RNR divisions and RN University units. Last seven craft have not been completed as builders are now in liquidation. Hulls towed to Portsmouth in late 1986 awaiting decision regarding their completion.

40

G. DAVIES

HMS Kingfisher

BIRD CLASS

Ship	Pennant Number	Completion Date	Builder
CORMORANT	P256	1976	James & Stone
HART	P257	1976	James & Stone
REDPOLE	P259	1970	Fairmile
KINGFISHER	P260	1975	R. Dunston
CYGNET	P261	1976	R. Dunston
PETEREL	P262	1976	R. Dunston
SANDPIPER	P263	1977	R. Dunston

Displacement 190 tons **Dimensions** 37m x 7m x 2m **Speed** 21 knots **Armament** 1 x 40mm gun **Complement** 24.

Notes
PETEREL and SANDPIPER are training ships attached to the Britannia Royal Naval College at Dartmouth. REDPOLE, HART and CORMORANT commissioned into the Royal Navy in 1985 after service as RAF search and rescue craft. HART & CORMORANT are smaller craft and are based at Gibraltar.

M. LOUAGIE

HMS Attacker

ATTACKER CLASS

Ship	Pennant Number	Completion Date	Builder
ATTACKER	P281	1983	Allday
CHASER	P282	1984	Allday
FENCER	P283	1983	Allday
HUNTER	P284	1983	Allday
STRIKER	P285	1984	Allday

Displacement 34 tons **Dimensions** 20m x 5m x 1m **Speed** 24 knots **Complement** 11.

Notes
Seamanship & Navigational training vessels for the Royal Naval Reserve & University RN Units. Based on a successful design used by HM Customs. Ships are based at Glasgow, Aberdeen, Southampton, London and Liverpool respectively.

● HMS OSPREY

HMS Mentor

Ship	Pennant Number	Completion Date	Builder
MANLY	A92	1982	R. Dunston
MENTOR	A94	1982	R. Dunston
MILBROOK	A97	1982	R. Dunston
MESSINA	A107	1982	R. Dunston

Displacement 127 tons **Dimensions** 25m x 6m x 2m **Speed** 10 knots **Complement** 13.

Notes
Very similar to the RMAS/RNXS tenders. These four craft are all employed on training duties (first three named attached to HMS RALEIGH for new entry training). IXWORTH (A318), ETTRICK (A274), ELSING (A277), IRONBRIDGE (A311) & DATCHET (A357) are all former RMAS tenders now flying the White Ensign.

43

HMS Roebuck

ROEBUCK CLASS

Ship	Pennant Number	Completion Date	Builder
ROEBUCK	A130	1986	Brooke Marine

Displacement 1500 tonnes **Dimensions** 64m x 13m x 4m **Speed** 15 knots **Complement** 47.

Notes

Carrying out trials during most of 1987. Will eventually replace one of the larger 'H' class vessels in the Survey Fleet.

HMS Herald

HECLA CLASS

Ship	Pennant Number	Completion Date	Builder
HECLA	A133	1965	Yarrow
HECATE	A137	1965	Yarrow
HERALD	A138	1974	Robb Caledon

Displacement 2,733 tons **Dimensions** 79m x 15m x 5m **Speed** 14 knots **Complement** 115.

Notes
Able to operate for long periods away from shore support, these ships and the smaller ships of the Hydrographic Fleet collect the data that is required to produce the Admiralty Charts and publications which are sold to mariners worldwide. Each ship usually carries a Wasp helicopter. HERALD is an improved version of the earlier ships and now operates mainly in the South Atlantic. In this role she is armed (2 x 20mm) and painted grey. HYDRA sold to Indonesia (1986). HECLA to be deleted in 1987. HECATE a year later.

S U R V E Y   S H I P S

HMS Fox

BULLDOG CLASS

Ship	Pennant Number	Completion Date	Builder
BULLDOG	A317	1968	Brooke Marine
BEAGLE	A319	1968	Brooke Marine
FOX	A320	1968	Brooke Marine
FAWN	A335	1968	Brooke Marine

Displacement 1,088 tons **Dimensions** 60m x 11m x 4m **Speed** 15 knots **Complement** 39.

Notes
Designed to operate in coastal waters.

● RNAS CULDROSE

HMS Challenger

SEABED OPERATIONS VESSEL

Ship	Pennant Number	Completion Date	Builder
CHALLENGER	K07	1984	Scott Lithgow

Displacement 6,400 tons **Dimensions** 134m x 18m x 5m **Speed** 15 knots **Complement** 185.

Notes
CHALLENGER is equipped to find, inspect and, where appropriate, recover objects from the seabed at greater depths than is currently possible. She is designed with a saturation diving system enabling up to 12 men to live in comfort for long periods in a decompression chamber amidships, taking their turns to be lowered in a diving bell to work on the seabed. Also fitted to carry out salvage work. Until CHALLENGER has completed lengthy trials, the MV SEAFORTH CLANSMAN (3,300 tons) will remain on charter to the MoD.

SPECIAL SHIPS

47

HMY Britannia

ROYAL YACHT

Ship	Pennant Number	Completion Date	Builder
BRITANNIA	A00	1954	J. Brown

Displacement 4,961 tons **Dimensions** 126m x 17m x 5m **Speed** 21 knots **Complement** 270.

Notes
Probably the best known ship in the Royal Navy, BRITANNIA was designed to be converted to a hospital ship in time of war but this conversion was not made during the Falklands crisis. Is available for use in NATO exercises when not on 'Royal' business. Normally to be seen in Portsmouth Harbour when not away on official duties. The only seagoing ship in the RN commanded by an Admiral. To be refitted, at Devonport, in 1987.

HMS Intrepid

HMS Tireless

HMS Chaser

HMS Dumbarton Castle

HMS Bristol

HMS Beagle

(L)HMS Diomede and (R)HMS Brave

HMS Beaver

HMS Endurance

ICE PATROL SHIP

Ship	Pennant Number	Completion Date	Builder
ENDURANCE (ex MV Anita Dan)	A171	1956	Krogerwerft Rendsburg

Displacement 3,600 tons **Dimensions** 93m x 14m x 5m **Speed** 14 knots **Armament** 2 x 20mm guns **Complement** 124.

Notes
Purchased from Denmark in 1967. ENDURANCE is painted brilliant red for easy identification in the ice of Antarctica where she spends 6 months of the year. Her role is to undertake oceanographic and hydrographic surveys in the area and support scientists working ashore. A small Royal Marine detachment is embarked. Was to have been "retired early" after her 1982 season in Antarctica, but reprieved as a result of the Falklands crisis. Refitted at Devonport 1986/7. New flight deck and hangar facilities for Lynx helicopters fitted.

● B. JONES

HMS Wakeful

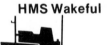

TUG/SUBMARINE TENDER

Ship	Pennant Number	Builder
WAKEFUL (Ex Dan)	A236	Cochranes

Displacement 900 tons **Dimensions** 44m x 11m x 5m **Speed** 14 knots **Complement** 25.

Notes
Purchased from Swedish owners in 1974 for duties in the Clyde area as Submarine Target Ship and at the Clyde Submarine Base —HMS NEPTUNE. Has been used for Fishery Protection work and the shadowing of Soviet warships in British waters.

MERCHANT SHIPS 'ON CHARTER' TO THE ROYAL NAVY

During the Falklands Crisis a considerable number of Merchant Ships were 'taken up from trade' to supplement the RN & RFA. A large number of these vessels remain working for the Ministry. Other merchant ships are employed in secondary support and training duties in home waters—frequently a most cost-effective way for the Navy to carry out these tasks.

IRISHMAN—one of the tugs on charter to the Royal Navy for Harbour duties in the Falklands.

M/V SEAFORTH CLANSMAN the Navy's temporary diving trials ship.

M/V NORTHELLA—the Navigational training ship.

Ships "taken up from trade" include the following ships:
ARCTIC FREEBOOTER, BON ESPRIT, BRITISH ESK, BRITISH TAMAR, EUROMAN, ICELARK, IRISHMAN, LUCERNA, MAERSK ASCENSION, MAERSK HARRIER, PROUD SEAHORSE, ST ANGUS.

THE NAVY'S MISSILES

SEA SKUA

An anti-surface ship missile. It is carried by the Lynx helicopter.

IKARA

A rocket propelled anti-submarine missile designed to deliver homing torpedoes. It is fitted in some Leander Class frigates.

SEACAT

A close-range anti-aircraft missile. Control is by radar tracking and visual guidance. Propulsion is by solid fuel. It is fitted in some frigates and destroyers and in HMS Hermes.

SEA DART

A ship-to-air medium-range missile with anti-ship capability. Propulsion is by ramjet and solid boost. It is carried in aircraft carriers and destroyers.

SEA WOLF

A high speed close-range anti-missile and anti-aircraft missile with fully automatic radar control and guidance. It is fitted in some frigates.

EXOCET

A medium-range surface-to-surface missile with a very low trajectory and a radar homing head. It is carried in some frigates and destroyers.

SIDEWINDER

An infra-red homing air-to-air missile. It has a solid propellant motor and a high explosive warhead. It is carried on the Sea Harrier.

SS 11

An anti-tank missile used in the Royal Marines Commando Wessex helicopters. It has a range of over 2,700 metres and can achieve a high degree of penetration.

AS 12

An air-to-surface wire-guided and spin-stabilised missile developed from the SS 11. It has a range of 6,000 metres.

SUB HARPOON

A long-range anti-ship missile launched from a submerged submarine. It is the principal anti-surface ship armament of the Fleet submarines.

STING-RAY

The most sophisticated homing torpedo in service. It can be fired from deck-mounted tubes or dropped by helicopter.

POLARIS

Submarine-launched ballistic missile fitted with nuclear warheads. It has a range of 2,500 nautical miles with solid-fuel propulsion.

THE ROYAL FLEET AUXILIARY

The Royal Fleet Auxiliary Service is operated by the Director of Supplies & Transport (Ships and Fuel) whose directorate forms part of the Royal Navy Supply and Transport Service (RNSTS) within the Ministry of Defence. The RNSTS provides the total logistic support of the Royal Navy and is civilian manned throughout under the management of the Director General of Supplies & Transport (Navy).

All Royal Fleet Auxiliaries are manned by merchant navy personnel and operate under their own distinctive flag—a blue ensign with a vertical anchor in gold on the fly, which distinguishes them from other non-commissioned ships and craft engaged in the naval service. All officers, and a growing proportion of ratings, serve under contract to the Royal Fleet Auxiliary Service.

The ships, all painted in standard RN grey, look far more businesslike than RFA's of a generation ago. The ships now look very much like warships and their merchant navy status has been difficult to maintain. It has been "in the wind" for some two years that the fleet would be "de-registered" and this is now proceeding—now that the normal lengthy round of consultations with the unions, Department of Transport and Lloyds have taken place.

Slowly, all RFA's will become government owned vessels—as much as they may look like warships (with a light armament and helicopters embarked in a large proportion of the fleet) the ships will still be inspected by Lloyds, acting as agents for MoD. Safety equipment checks will still be to Merchant Navy standards. The main worries within the RFA seem to be on the accommodation front—over the years the unions have agreed high standards of accommodation with the MoD for RFA personnel at sea. Whilst the accommodation standards in the current fleet cannot alter much it will be interesting to see if these same standards are incorporated into "new build" ships.

Since the last issue of this book a firm order has been placed for a single "Auxiliary oiler replenishment" (AOR) to give it its correct Nato tally. In plain language, the new ship will be a combined tanker and stores ship. A few years ago the word was that ten would eventually be ordered—the figure is hardly mentioned today and with a price tag of £130 million each, and stores to the value of £150 million needed to fill her one has to be more than an optimist to see an order for anything approaching ten ever being placed.

Whilst the AOR will have a major role to play in operations with a task group there are many other commitments carried out by the Royal Navy today which are basically one or two ship operations. All need RFA support. The Armilla, Falklands and North Atlantic patrols, and West Indies Guardship all spring to mind. Today, these commitments are supported by the faithful Rover and Larger Ol and Tide Class tankers. All these ships are of basic 1960's design and have been worked far harder than warships of that vintage. Very soon they will all need replacing and an AOR would be a totally non cost effective ship for all these smaller, routine, commitments the navy has worldwide. The commitments will doubtless change over the years but others will, no doubt, replace them.

With the British shipbuilders SSK20 design the commercial sector came up with an adequate "Multi-Role" ship that would fulfil most of the Navy's requirements for the support of a small group of ships. With a £60 million estimated cost there are plenty of senior officers who would opt for the cheaper vessel—if they could be promised more hulls! If orders are not placed shortly the surface fleet in years to come is not going to be able to operate far from home—or perhaps that is all part of the "Masterplan" for the Royal Navy of the nineties anyway!

Whilst experts are still sucking their teeth at the money that was wasted on RFA RELIANT (only for her to be sold off at a knockdown price as a nine year old ship.) The navy has certainly lost a major hull that could have been given a wide range of aviation and/or training roles.

The arrival of RFA ARGUS into service is, however, a jewel in the RFA's crown. No doubt many an RN officer would love to be offered the command but the largest ship in the MoD's fleet will fly the blue ensign of the RFA. As the RFA's ships become larger—and their roles far more military than they were just 5-10 years ago it will be interesting to see if and when new ships are ordered to replace FEARLESS and INTREPID they too are "flagged out" to the RFA.

As the RFA becomes much more a part of the Royal Navy (as much as the Submarine service and Fleet Air Arm are large, partially independant, subdivisions of the overall "firm") it is frequently heard within the Ministry and onboard RFA's at sea that the time has come for the management to be a professional naval management similar to Flag Officers of the navies various commands. It seems that the current civil service management—in which executives frequently come from other corners of the civil service for just a couple of years—cannot be in the best interests of the RFA—or the Royal Navy.

The civil service have, in the main, served the RFA well in the past but with the best will in the world are not totally suited to managing the fleet of the nineties. How any changes can be made, with everyone fighting to maintain their 'career structures', is not easy to see. No doubt, without firm directives 'from above' little *will* change.

SHIPS OF THE ROYAL FLEET AUXILIARY
Pennant Numbers

Ship	Penn. No.	Ship	Penn. No.
TIDESPRING	A75	GOLD ROVER	A271
APPLELEAF	A79	BLACK ROVER	A273
BRAMBLELEAF	A81	FORT GRANGE	A385
BAYLEAF	A109	FORT AUSTIN	A386
ORANGELEAF	A110	RESOURCE	A480
OAKLEAF	A111	REGENT	A486
OLWEN	A122	ENGADINE	K08
OLNA	A123	SIR BEDIVERE	L3004
OLMEDA	A124	SIR GALAHAD	L3005
DILIGENCE	A132	SIR GERAINT	L3027
ARGUS	A135	SIR LANCELOT	L3029
GREEN ROVER	A268	SIR PERCIVALE	L3036
GREY ROVER	A269	SIR TRISTRAM	L3505
BLUE ROVER	A270	SIR CARADOC	L3522

● P. COWFEE

RFA Olna

'OL' CLASS

Ship	Pennant Number	Completion Date	Builder
OLWEN	A122	1965	Hawthorn Leslie
OLNA	A123	1966	Hawthorn Leslie
OLMEDA	A124	1965	Swan Hunter

Displacement 36,000 tons **Dimensions** 197m x 26m x 10m **Speed** 19 knots **Complement** 94.

Notes
These ships can operate up to 3 Sea King helicopters. Dry stores can be carried—and transferred at sea—as well as a wide range of fuel, aviation spirit and lubricants.

T
A
N
K
E
R
S

RFA Tidespring

TIDE CLASS

Ship	Pennant Number	Completion Date	Builder
TIDESPRING	A75	1963	Hawthorn Leslie

Displacement 27,400 tons **Dimensions** 177m x 22m x 10m **Speed** 18 knots **Complement** 110.

Notes
Built to fuel warships at sea in any part of the world including strengthening for ice operations. A hangar and flight deck provides space for three Sea King helicopters if required. Was due to be "retired early" during 1982/3 but reprieved for Falklands crisis and remains in service..

● C. NORTH

RFA Gold Rover

ROVER CLASS

Ship	Pennant Number	Completion Date	Builder
GREEN ROVER	A268	1969	Swan Hunter
GREY ROVER	A269	1970	Swan Hunter
BLUE ROVER	A270	1970	Swan Hunter
GOLD ROVER	A271	1974	Swan Hunter
BLACK ROVER	A273	1974	Swan Hunter

Displacement 11,522 tons **Dimensions** 141m x 19m x 7m **Speed** 18 knots **Complement** 50.

Notes
Small Fleet Tankers designed to supply HM ships with fresh water, dry cargo and refrigerated provisions as well as a range of fuel and lubricants. Helicopter deck but no hangar.

● R.S. NEED

RFA Appleleaf

LEAF CLASS

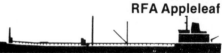

Ship	Pennant Number	Completion Date	Builder
APPLELEAF	A79	1980	Cammell Laird
BRAMBLELEAF	A81	1980	Cammell Laird
BAYLEAF	A109	1982	Cammell Laird
ORANGELEAF	A110	1982	Cammell Laird
OAKLEAF	A111	1981	Uddevalla

Displacement 37,747 tons **Dimensions** 170m x 26m x 12m **Speed** 14.5 knots **Complement** 60.

Notes
All are ex merchant ships either purchased or chartered by MoD. OAKLEAF (ex OKTANIA) differs from the other ships of the class which are all commercial Stat 32 tankers. At 49,310 tons she is the largest vessel in RFA/RN service. The old tankers PEARLEAF and PLUMLEAF have now been returned to their owners.

● T. HARDING   **RFA Fort Austin**

FORT CLASS

Ship	Pennant Number	Completion Date	Builder
FORT GRANGE	A385	1978	Scott Lithgow
FORT AUSTIN	A386	1979	Scott Lithgow

Displacement 17,000 tons **Dimensions** 183m x 24m x 9m **Speed** 20 knots **Complement** 133.

Notes
Full hangar and maintenance facilities are provided and up to four Sea King helicopters can be carried for both the transfer of stores and anti-submarine protection of a group of ships. Both are armed when in the South Atlantic. 2 x 20mm guns are mounted on the Scot platforms.

RFA Regent

REGENT CLASS

Ship	Pennant Number	Completion Date	Builder
RESOURCE	A480	1967	Scotts
REGENT	A486	1967	Harland & Wolff

Displacement 22,890 **Dimensions** 195m x 24m x 8m **Speed** 21 knots **Complement** 123.

Notes
The widest range of naval armament stores are carried onboard plus a limited range of general naval stores and food. A ships flight (Wessex 5) is permanently embarked.

68

RFA Sir Bedivere

LANDING SHIPS
SIR LANCELOT CLASS

Ship	Pennant Number	Completion Date	Builder
SIR BEDIVERE	L3004	1967	Hawthorn
SIR GERAINT	L3027	1967	Stephen
SIR LANCELOT	L3029	1964	Fairfield
SIR PERCIVALE	L3036	1968	Hawthorn
SIR TRISTRAM	L3505	1967	Hawthorn

Displacement 5,550 tons **Dimensions** 126m x 18m x 4m **Speed** 17 knots **Armament** Can be fitted with 2 x 40mm guns in emergency **Complement** 69.

Notes
Manned by the RFA but tasked by the Army, these ships are used for heavy transport of stores—embarked by bow and stern doors —and beach assault landings. Can operate helicopters from tank deck if required. SIR TRISTRAM was rebuilt at a cost of £13m during 1983-5 as a result of Falklands War damage, a 29′ section being inserted amidships and all aluminium superstructure replaced by steel. A replacement for her sister ship—SIR GALAHAD—was launched on the Tyne in late 1986.

S
P
E
C
I
A
L

S
H
I
P
S

69

RFA Sir Caradoc

Ship	Pennant Number	Completion Date	Builder
SIR CARADOC	L3522	1973	Trosvik Verksted

Displacement 3,350 tons **Dimensions** 124m x 16 **Speed** 14 knots
Complement 24

Notes
Chartered as a stop gap replacement for RFA SIR GALAHAD.
   Found to be unsuitable for the South Atlantic and mainly
employed on the Marchwood/Antwerp freight run for MoD (Army).

● FPS FALKLAND ISLANDS

RFA Diligence

Ship	Pennant Number	Completion Date	Builder
DILIGENCE	A132	1981	Oresundsvarvet

Displacement 5,814 tons **Dimensions** 120m x 12m **Speed** 15 knots
Complement RFA 40. RN Personnel — approx 100.

Notes
Formerly the M/V Stena Inspector purchased (£25m) for service in the South Atlantic. Accommodation is provided for a 100 man Fleet Maintenance Unit. Her deep diving complex has been removed & workshops added. Due to refit in UK during 1987. Her place being taken in the South Atlantic by M/V Stena Seaspread—on charter.

● ARTISTS IMPRESSION   **RFA Argus**

Ship	Pennant Number	Completion Date	Builder
ARGUS	A135	1981	Cantieri Navali Breda

Displacement 28,063 tons (full load) **Dimensions** 175m x 30m x 8m **Speed** 18 knots **Armament** 4 x 30mm. 2 x 20mm **Complement** 254 (inc 137 Air Group) **Aircraft** 6 Sea King.

Notes
Formerly the M/V CONTENDER BEZANT taken up from trade during the Falklands crisis. Purchased in 1984 (£13 million) for conversion to an 'Aviation Training Ship'. A £50 million re-build was undertaken at Belfast from 1984-86. She will replace ENGADINE in Autumn 1987 and be based at Portland.

72

● HMS OSPREY

RFA Engadine

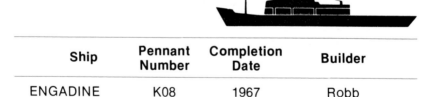

Ship	Pennant Number	Completion Date	Builder
ENGADINE	K08	1967	Robb

Displacement 9,000 tons **Dimensions** 129m x 17m x 7m **Speed** 16 knots **Complement** 73 (+ RN group).

Notes
Specially built for RFA service (but with embarked RN personnel) to provide training ship for helicopter crews operating in deep waters well away from coasts. Can operate up to 6 helicopters and often embarks pilotless target aircraft for exercises. Hangar for them above main hangar. Will be deleted from the RFA Fleet when ARGUS is operational.

ROYAL MARITIME
AUXILIARY SERVICE

The Royal Maritime Auxiliary Service Fleet is comprised of over 500 hulls, of which 310 are self propelled, including small harbour launches, the remainder being dumb craft such as lighters etc. It is administered by the Director of Marine Services (Naval) to whom the Captains of the Ports and Resident Naval Officers at the various Naval Bases are mainly responsible for the provision of Marine Services to the Royal Navy. The RMAS also provides many types of craft for the numerous and diverse requirements of other Ministry of Defence departments.

Ships of the RMAS, which can be seen at work in all the Naval Bases throughout the United Kingdom and at Gibraltar, are easily identified by their black hulls, buff coloured superstructure and funnels, and by the RMAS flag, which is a blue ensign defaced in the fly by a yellow anchor over two wavy lines. Pennant numbers are painted only on those vessels that are normally employed outside harbour limits.

● A. MASON

Dog Class Tugs in formation at Faslane

The largest section of the fleet is employed on harbour duties, the types of vessels involved being Berthing and Tractor Tugs, Fleet Tenders, Tank Cleaning Lighters, Harbour Launches, Naval Armament Vessels and dumb lighters for carrying explosive stores, general stores, fuel, water and victuals to the Royal Navy, NATO Navies and Royal Fleet Auxiliary ships when they are in port or at anchor. In keeping with the Director of Marine Services policy of multi-role vessels, many of the larger units of the fleet have been modified to back up the harbour fleet when required.

A smaller section of the fleet is, however, engaged in a purely sea-going capacity. Ocean Tugs, Torpedo Recovery Vessels and Mooring and Salvage Vessels are designed and equipped for world wide towing and complex Marine Salvage operations. Experimental Trials Vessels, fitted with some of the most sophisticated modern equipment, are deployed on a wide range of duties in the fast growing area of advanced experimental technology necessary for the design of new warships, weapon systems and machinery.

Problems associated with the control and treatment of oil pollution at sea have become more pressing in recent years. To deal with emergencies in Dockyard Ports and to assist the Department of Transport with those that may arise around the coastline of the United Kingdom, the RMAS has adapted many of its vessels to carry chemical dispersants and the necessary spraying equipment.

The size and composition of the RMAS Fleet is under constant review to ensure its compatability with the changing requirements of the Royal Navy, which it exists to serve. Older units are being phased out, at times without replacement and the introduction of new more versatile vessels will continue to provide savings in the total number of ships required and the manpower required to operate them.

Pressure has increased over recent years in all areas of Defence Expenditure to obtain the best possible value for money in the interests of maintaining "the teeth" at maximum efficiency. It is inevitable therefore that much of the pressure falls upon the support area in which the Marine Services play a vital part.

The task of reviewing the recent audit is still continuing. However, Harbour berthing/mooring and associated activities, together with the support of the RNXS, will remain "in house". The remainder of the services provided by the RMAS are still "under review".

However, it should be stated that the professional standards achieved by the Marine Services are second to none, and are held in high regard by all its customers. The chief concern of DMS(N) is to preserve the services provided to the Fleet and his other customers in the most cost effective way and without loss of operational flexibility. An extra ordinary length of time has now passed whilst the future of the RMAS has been under the microscope. Hopefully, for the men involved whose careers are in the balance, a decision one way or the other will be made before the next edition of this book is published. At the time of publishing it looked as if this lengthy and costly exercise was only producing a 5% reduction of seagoing manpower—and, at the end of the day, no great change in the current status quo will be seen.

SHIPS OF THE ROYAL MARITIME AUXILIARY SERVICE — PENNANT NUMBERS

Ship	Penn. No.	Ship	Penn. No.
MELTON	A83	KATHLEEN	A166
MENAI	A84	EXPRESS	A167
MEON	A87	LABRADOR	A168
MILFORD	A91	KITTY	A170
TYPHOON	A95	LESLEY	A172
BEAULIEU	A99	DOROTHY	A173
BEMBRIDGE	A101	LILAH	A174
BLAKENEY	A104	MARY	A175
ALSATIAN	A106	EDITH	A177
FELICITY	A112	HUSKY	A178
MAGNET	A114	MASTIFF	A180
LODESTONE	A115	IRENE	A181
CAIRN	A126	SALUKI	A182
TORRENT	A127	ISABEL	A183
TORRID	A128	SALMOOR	A185
DALMATION	A129	SALMASTER	A186
TORNADO	A140	SALMAID	A187
TORCH	A141	POINTER	A188
TORMENTOR	A142	SETTER	A189
TOREADOR	A143	JOAN	A190
DAISY	A145	JOYCE	A193
WATERMAN	A146	GWENDOLINE	A196
FRANCES	A147	SEALYHAM	A197
FIONA	A148	HELEN	A198
FLORENCE	A149	MYRTLE	A199
GENEVIEVE	A150	SPANIEL	A201
GEORGINA	A152	NANCY	A202
EXAMPLE	A153	NORAH	A205
EXPLORER	A154	LLANDOVERY	A207
DEERHOUND	A155	LAMLASH	A208
DAPHNE	A156	CHARLOTTE	A210
LOYAL HELPER	A157	LECHLADE	A211
SUPPORTER	A158	ENDEAVOUR	A213
LOYAL WATCHER	A159	BEE	A216
LOYAL VOLUNTEER	A160	CHRISTINE	A217
LOYAL MEDIATOR	A161	LOYAL MODERATOR	A220
ELKHOUND	A162	FORCEFUL	A221
EXPLOIT	A163	NIMBLE	A222
GOOSANDER	A164	POWERFUL	A223
POCHARD	A165		

Ship	Penn. No.	Ship	Penn. No.
ADEPT	A224	CRICCIETH	A391
BUSTLER	A225	GLENCOE	A392
CAPABLE	A226	DUNSTER	A393
CAREFUL	A227	FINTRY	A394
FAITHFUL	A228	GRASMERE	A402
CRICKET	A229	KINLOSS	A482
COCKCHAFER	A230	CROMARTY	A488
DEXTEROUS	A231	DORNOCH	A490
GNAT	A239	ROLLICKER	A502
SHEEPDOG	A250	HEADCORN	A1766
LYDFORD	A251	HEVER	A1767
DORIS	A252	HARLECH	A1768
LADYBIRD	A253	HAMBLEDON	A1769
MEAVEY	A254	LOYAL	
CICALA	A263	CHANCELLOR	A1770
SCARAB	A272	LOYAL PROCTOR	A1771
KINBRACE	A281	HOLMWOOD	A1772
AURICULA	A285	HORNING	A1773
ILCHESTER	A308	MANDARIN	P192
INSTOW	A309	PINTAIL	P193
FOXHOUND	A326	GARGANEY	P194
BASSET	A327	GOLDENEYE	P195
COLLIE	A328	ALNMOUTH	Y13
CORGI	A330	WATERFALL	Y17
FOTHERBY	A341	WATERSHED	Y18
FELSTEAD	A348	WATERSPOUT	Y19
CARTMEL	A350	WATERSIDE	Y20
ELKSTONE	A353	OILPRESS	Y21
FROXFIELD	A354	OILSTONE	Y22
EPWORTH	A355	OILWELL	Y23
DATCHET	A357	OILFIELD	Y24
ROYSTERER	A361	OILBIRD	Y25
DOLWEN	A362	OILMAN	Y26
DENMEAD	A363	WATERCOURSE	Y30
WHITEHEAD	A364	WATERFOWL	Y31
FULBECK	A365		
ROBUST	A366		
NEWTON	A367		
KINTERBURY	A378		
THROSK	A379		
CRICKLADE	A381		
CLOVELLY	A389		

RMAS Roysterer

ROYSTERER CLASS

Ship	Pennant Number	Completion Date	Builder
ROYSTERER	A361	1972	C.D. Holmes
ROBUST	A366	1974	C.D. Holmes
ROLLICKER	A502	1973	C.D. Holmes

G.R.T. 1,036 tons **Dimensions** 54m x 12m x 6m **Speed** 15 knots **Complement** 28.

Notes
Built for salvage and long range towage, but are also used for various "deepwater" trials.

78

● HMS OSPREY

RMAS Typhoon

TYPHOON CLASS

Ship	Pennant Number	Completion Date	Builder
TYPHOON	A95	1960	Henry Robb

G.R.T. 1,034 tons **Dimensions** 60m x 12m x 4m **Speed** 17 knots **Complement** 27.

Notes
Long range towage and salvage tug. Now laid up, at Portsmouth, in reserve.

79

T U G S

R. DUNSTON

RMAS Dexterous

HARBOUR TUGS
TWIN UNIT TRACTOR TUGS (TUTT'S)

Ship	Pennant Number	Completion Date	Builder
FORCEFUL	A221	1985	R. Dunston
NIMBLE	A222	1985	R. Dunston
POWERFUL	A223	1985	R. Dunston
ADEPT	A224	1980	R. Dunston
BUSTLER	A225	1981	R. Dunston
CAPABLE	A226	1981	R. Dunston
CAREFUL	A227	1982	R. Dunston
FAITHFUL	A228	1985	R. Dunston
DEXTEROUS	A231	1986	R. Dunston

G.R.T. 375 tons **Dimensions** 39m x 10m x 4m **Speed** 12 knots
Complement 10

Notes
The main harbour tug in naval service. Capable is at Gibraltar.

M. LENNON

RMAS Sealyham

DOG CLASS

Ship	Penn. No.	Ship	Penn. No.
ALSATIAN	A106	POINTER	A188
CAIRN ●	A126	SETTER	A189
DALMATIAN	A129	SEALYHAM	A197
DEERHOUND	A155	SPANIEL	A201
ELKHOUND	A162	SHEEPDOG	A250
LABRADOR	A168	FOXHOUND	A326
HUSKY	A178	BASSET	A327
MASTIFF	A180	COLLIE ●	A328
SALUKI	A182	CORGI	A330

G.R.T. 152 tons **Dimensions** 29m x 8m x 4m **Speed** 12 knots **Complement** 8

Notes
General harbour tugs — all completed between 1962 & 1972.
● No longer tugs. Refitted as trials vessels for service at Kyle of Lochalsh.

AUTHOR'S PHOTO

RMAS Doris

IMPROVED GIRL CLASS

Ship	Penn. No.	Ship	Penn. No.
DAISY	A145	CHARLOTTE	A210
DAPHNE	A156	CHRISTINE	A217
DOROTHY	A173	DORIS	A252
EDITH	A177		

G.R.T. 75 tons **Speed** 10 knots **Complement** 4

Notes
All completed 1971-2.

M. LOUAGIE

RMAS Joan

IRENE CLASS

Ship	Penn. No.	Ship	Penn. No.
KATHLEEN	A166	ISABEL	A183
KITTY	A170	JOAN	A190
LESLEY	A172	JOYCE	A193
LILAH	A174	MYRTLE	A199
MARY	A175	NANCY	A202
IRENE	A181	NORAH	A205

G.R.T. 89 tons **Speed** 8 knots **Complement** 4

Notes
Known as Water Tractors these craft are used for basin moves and towage of light barges.

S. GOODMAN

RMAS Frances

FELICITY CLASS

Ship	Penn. No.	Ship	Penn. No.
FELICITY	A112	GENEVIEVE	A150
FRANCES	A147	GEORGINA	A152
FIONA	A148	GWENDOLINE	A196
FLORENCE	A149	HELEN	A198

G.R.T. 80 tons **Speed** 10 knots **Complement** 4

Notes
Water Tractors — completed in 1973; FRANCES, FLORENCE &
GENEVIEVE completed 1980.

M. LENNON

RMAS Whitehead

TRIALS SHIPS

Ship	Pennant Number	Completion Date	Builder
WHITEHEAD	A364	1971	Scotts

G.R.T. 3,427 tons **Dimensions** 97m x 15m x 5m **Speed** 15.5 knots **Complement** 50

Notes
Fitted with Torpedo Tubes for trial firings. Long term future under discussion within MoD. Not fully employed as a Torpedo trials vessel and may replace ABDIEL in MCM role.

RMAS Newton

Ship	Pennant Number	Completion Date	Builder
NEWTON	A367	1976	Scotts

G.R.T. 2,779 tons **Dimensions** 99m x 16m x 6m **Speed** 15 knots
Complement 52

Notes
Built as sonar propagation trials ship but can also be used as a
Cable Layer.

86

RMAS Auricula

TEST & EXPERIMENTAL SONAR TENDER

Ship	Pennant Number	Completion Date	Builder
AURICULA	A285	1981	Ferguson Bros

G.R.T. 981 tons **Dimensions** 52m x 11m x 3m **Speed** 12 knots
Complement 22

Notes
Employed on evaluation work of new sonar equipment that may
equip RN ships of the future.

M. LENNON

RMAS Kinterbury

ARMAMENT STORES CARRIERS

Ship	Pennant Number	Completion Date	Builder
KINTERBURY	A378	1980	Appledore SB
THROSK	A379	1977	Cleland SB Co.

G.R.T. 1,357 tons **Dimensions** 64m x 12m x 5m **Speed** 14 knots **Complement** 24

Notes
2 holds carry Naval armament stores, ammunition and guided missiles. KINTERBURY varies slightly from earlier sister ship. One ship is normally operational—the other in reserve. The Army's Armament Stores Carrier ST GEORGE is very similar.

88

M. LENNON

RMAS Bee

INSECT CLASS

Ship	Pennant Number	Completion Date	Builder
BEE	A216	1970	C.D. Holmes
CRICKET	A229	1972	Beverley
COCKCHAFER	A230	1971	Beverley
GNAT	A239	1972	Beverley
LADYBIRD	A253	1973	Beverley
CICALA	A263	1971	Beverley
SCARAB	A272	1973	Beverley

G.R.T. 279 tons **Dimensions** 34m x 8m x 3m **Speed** 10.5 knots **Complement** 7-13

Notes
SCARAB is fitted as a Mooring Vessel and COCKCHAFER as a Stores Carrier — remainder are Naval Armament carriers.

TENDERS

RNXS Loyal Volunteer

LOYAL CLASS

Ship	Penn. No.	Ship	Penn. No.
LOYAL HELPER	A157	LOYAL MEDIATOR	A161
SUPPORTER	A158	LOYAL MODERATOR	A220
LOYAL WATCHER	A159	LOYAL CHANCELLOR	A1770
LOYAL VOLUNTEER	A160	LOYAL PROCTOR	A1771

G.R.T. 112 tons **Dimensions** 24m x 6m x 3m **Speed** 10.5 knots
Complement 24

Notes
All these craft are operated by the Royal Naval Auxiliary Service (RNXS) — men (and women) — who in time of emergency would man these craft for duties as port control vessels.

90

● RNAS CULDROSE

RMAS Fulbeck

(TYPE A, B & X) TENDERS

Ship	Penn. No.	Ship	Penn. No.
MELTON	A83	CRICKLADE	A381
MENAI	A84	CLOVELLY	A389
MEON	A87	CRICCIETH	A391
MILFORD	A91	GLENCOE	A392
LLANDOVERY	A207	DUNSTER	A393
LAMLASH	A208	FINTRY	A394
LECHLADE	A211	GRASMERE	A402
LYDFORD	A251	CROMARTY	A488
MEAVEY	A254	DORNOCH	A490
ILCHESTER*	A308	HEADCORN	A1766
INSTOW*	A309	HEVER	A1767
FOTHERBY	A341	HARLECH	A1768
FELSTEAD	A348	HAMBLEDON	A1769
ELKSTONE	A353	HOLMWOOD	A1772
FROXFIELD	A354	HORNING	A1773
EPWORTH	A355		
DENMEAD	A363	DATCHET	A357
FULBECK	A365		

G.R.T. 78 tons **Dimensions** 24m x 6m x 3m **Speed** 10.5 knots **Complement** 5

Notes
All completed since 1971 to replace Motor Fishing Vessels. Vessels marked* are diving tenders. Remainder are Training Tenders, Passenger Ferries, or Cargo Vessels. DATCHET (A357) is a diving tender—not of this class but similar—based at Devonport with an RN crew. LYDFORD formerly HMS VIGILANT; MEAVEY—HMS ALERT.

RMAS Blakeney

ABERDOVEY CLASS ('63 DESIGN)

Ship	Penn. No.	Ship	Penn. No.
ALNMOUTH	Y13	BLAKENEY ●	A104
BEAULIEU ●	A99	CARTMEL	A350
BEMBRIDGE	A101		

G.R.T. 77 tons **Dimensions** 24m x 5m x 3m **Speed** 10.5 knots
Complement 5

Notes
ALNMOUTH is a Sea Cadet Training Ship based at Plymouth,
BEMBRIDGE at Portsmouth. ABERDOVEY, ABINGER, APPLEBY,
BEDDGELERT and BIBURY no longer on the RMAS Fleet list.
Transfered/sold to various Sea Cadet Units.
● In service as Harbour tenders at Port Stanley with RN crews.

92

W. SARTORI

XSV Explorer

COASTAL TRAINING CRAFT
EXAMPLE CLASS

Ship	Pennant Number	Completion Date	Builder
XSV EXAMPLE	A153	1985	Watercraft
XSV EXPLORER	A154	1985	Watercraft
XSV EXPLOIT	A163		
XSV EXPRESS	A167		

Displacement 43 tons **Dimensions** 20m x 6m x 1m **Speed** 20 knots **Armament** Nil **Complement** 14

Notes
Should have replaced the former Inshore Minesweepers in RNXS service. The last two not completed due to the failure of the builders. At Portsmouth (late 1986) awaiting new contract for completion. The former Inshore Minesweeper PORTISHAM retained for service until new vessels completed.

RMAS Oilstone

OILPRESS CLASS

Ship	Pennant Number	Completion Date	Builder
OILPRESS	Y21	1969	Appledore Shipbuilders
OILSTONE	Y22	1969	" "
OILWELL	Y23	1969	" "
OILFIELD	Y24	1969	" "
OILBIRD	Y25	1969	" "
OILMAN	Y26	1969	" "

G.R.T. 362 tons **Dimensions** 41m x 9m x 3m **Speed** 11 knots
Complement 8

Notes
Employed as Harbour and Coastal Oilers.

R. WALKER   **RMAS Waterfall**

WATER CARRIERS
WATER CLASS

Ship	Pennant Number	Completion Date	Builder
WATERFALL	Y17	1967	Drypool Eng Co
WATERSHED	Y18	1967	Drypool Eng Co
WATERSPOUT	Y19	1967	Drypool Eng Co
WATERSIDE	Y20	1968	Drypool Eng Co
WATERCOURSE	Y30	1974	Drypool Eng Co
WATERFOWL	Y31	1974	Drypool Eng Co
WATERMAN	A146	1978	R. Dunston

G.R.T. 263 tons **Dimensions** 40m x 8m x 2m **Speed** 11 knots **Complement** 8

Notes
Capable of coastal passages, these craft normally supply either demineralised or fresh water to the Fleet within port limits.

95

M. LENNON

RMAS Lodestone

DEGAUSSING VESSELS
MAGNET CLASS

Ship	Pennant Number	Completion Date	Builder
MAGNET	A114	1979	Cleland
LODESTONE	A115	1980	Cleland

G.R.T. 828 tons **Dimensions** 55m x 12m x 4m **Speed** 14 knots **Complement** 10

Notes
One ship is normally operational, the other kept in reserve.

M. LENNON

RMAS Torrid

TORPEDO RECOVERY VESSELS (TRV'S)
TORRID CLASS

Ship	Pennant Number	Completion Date	Builder
TORRENT	A127	1971	Cleland SB Co
TORRID	A128	1972	Cleland SB Co

G.R.T. 550 tons **Dimensions** 46m x 9m x 3m **Speed** 12 knots
Complement 18

Notes
A stern ramp is built for the recovery of torpedoes fired for trials
and exercises. A total of 32 can be carried.

A. DENHOLM   **RMAS Toreador**

TORNADO CLASS

Ship	Pennant Number	Completion Date	Builder
TORNADO	A140	1979	Hall Russell
TORCH	A141	1980	Hall Russell
TORMENTOR	A142	1980	Hall Russell
TOREADOR	A143	1980	Hall Russell

G.R.T. 560 tons **Dimensions** 47m x 8m x 3m **Speed** 14 knots **Complement** 14

Notes
TORCH is based at Portland, TORMENTOR at Plymouth — remainder on the Clyde.

RMAS Salmoor

SAL CLASS

Ship	Pennant Number	Completion Date	Builder
SALMOOR	A185	1985	Hall Russell
SALMASTER	A186	1986	Hall Russell
SALMAID	A187	1986	Hall Russell

Displacement 2200 tonnes **Dimensions** 77m x 15m x 4m **Speed** 15 knots **Complement** 32

Notes
Built at a cost of £9 million each these ships have replaced the 40-year-old Kin class. They are multi-purpose vessels designed to lay and maintain underwater targets and moorings and undertake a wide range of salvage tasks.

M
S
V
'
S

R. WALKER

RMAS Goldeneye

WILD DUCK CLASS

Ship	Pennant Number	Completion Date	Builder
MANDARIN	P192	1964	C. Laird
PINTAIL	P193	1964	C. Laird
GARGANEY	P194	1966	Brooke Marine
GOLDENEYE	P195	1966	Brooke Marine
GOOSANDER	A164	1973	Robb Caledon
POCHARD	A165	1973	Robb Caledon

G.R.T. 900 tons* **Dimensions** 58mm x 12m x 4m **Speed** 10 knots
Complement 23-26
* Vessels vary slightly

Notes
Vessels capable of carrying out a wide range of duties laying moorings and heavy lift salvage work. 50 tons can be lifted over the horns and 200 tons over the bow.

RMAS Kinloss

KIN CLASS

Ship	Pennant Number	Completion Date	Builder
KINBRACE	A281	1944	A. Hall Aberdeen
KINLOSS	A482	1945	A. Hall Aberdeen

Displacement 1,050 tons **Dimensions** 54m x 11m x 4m **Speed** 9 knots **Complement** 23-26

Notes
Coastal Salvage Vessels re-engined between 1963 & 1967. KINBRACE is now in reserve at Portsmouth and KINLOSS has a trials role at Rosyth.

M. LENNON

RMAS Dolwen

DOLWEN CLASS

Ship	Pennant Number	Completion Date	Builder
DOLWEN (ex Hector Gulf)	A362	1962	P.K. Harris

Displacement 602 tons **Dimensions** 41m x 9m x 4m **Speed** 14 knots **Complement** 12

Notes
Built as a stern trawler, then purchased for use as a Buoy tender — now used as Safety Vessel for RAE ABERPORTH (S. Wales) from her base at Pembroke Dock. A contract is expected to be placed shortly for a purpose built replacement vessel to be built. ENDEAVOUR is a Torpedo Recovery/Trials Vessel at Portland.

G. DAVIES   **HMAV Arakan**

ARMY LANDING CRAFT

LCL CLASS   LANDING CRAFT LOGISTIC

Vessel	Pennant Number	Completion Date	Builder
HMAV Ardennes	L4001	1977	Brooke Marine
HMAV Arakan	L4003	1978	Brooke Marine

Displacement 1,050 tons **Dimensions** 72m x 15m x 2m **Speed** 10 knots **Complement** 35

Notes
Designed to carry up to 350 tons — up to Five Chieftain tanks — loaded onto open beaches through bow doors. Both are mainly used for missile transportation to the Royal Artillery ranges in the Outer Hebrides.

M. LOUAGIE

RCTV Andalsnes

RCL CLASS   RAMPED CRAFT LOGISTIC

Vessel	Pennant Number	Completion Date	Builder
RCTV Arromanches	L105	1981	Brooke Marine
RCTV Antwerp	L106	1981	Brooke Marine
RCTV Andalsnes	L107	1984	James & Stone
RCTV Abbeville	L108	1985	James & Stone
RCTV Akyab	L109	1985	James & Stone
RCTV Aachen	L110	1986	McTay Marine
RCTV Arezzo	L111	1986	McTay Marine
RCTV Agheila	L112	1987	McTay Marine
RCTV Audemer	L113	1987	McTay Marine

Displacement 165 tons **Dimensions** 30m x 8m x 2m **Speed** 9 knots
Complement 6

Notes
Smaller—"all purpose" landing craft capable of carrying up to
100 tons. In service in coastal waters around Cyprus, Hong Kong
& UK.

AIRCRAFT OF THE FLEET AIR ARM

Sea Harrier

British Aerospace Sea Harrier

Variants: FRS 1 (FRS 2 undergoing development 1987/88)
Role: Short take off, vertical landing (STOVL) fighter, reconnaissence and strike aircraft.
Engine: 1 x 21,500lb thrust Rolls Royce PEGASUS 104 turbojet.
Span 25′3″ **length** 47′7″ **height** 12′0″ **max weight** 26,200lb.
Max speed Mach 1.2 **Crew** 1 pilot.
Avionics: Blue Fox pulse radar. (To be replaced by the Blue Vixen pulse doppler radar in the FRS 2).
Armament: SEA EAGLE air to surface missiles. SIDEWINDER air to air missiles. (FRS 2 to carry the new Anglo/US AMRAAM radar guided air to air missiles). 2 x 30mm Aden cannons with 120 rounds per gun in detachable pods, one either side of the lower fuselage. 1 fuselage centreline and 4 underwing hardpoints. The inner wing stations are capable of carrying 2,000lb of stores and are plumbed for drop tanks. The other positions can carry stores up to 1,000lb in weight. Possible loads include 1,000lb, 500lb or practice bombs; BL 755 cluster bombs, Lepus flares, 190 or 100 gallon drop tanks. A single F95 camera is mounted obliquely in the nose for the reconnaissence role.
Squadron Service: 800, 801 and 899 squadrons in commission.
Notes: During 1987, 800 squadron will be embarked in HMS ILLUSTRIOUS and 801 in HMS ARK ROYAL. 899 squadron is responsible for the training of replacement pilots and the development of tactics and is normally shore based at RNAS YEOVILTON. In a period of tension it could embark to reinforce the embarked air groups in the carriers.

Westland SEA KING

Developed for the Royal Navy from the Sikorsky SH3D, the basic Seaking airframe is used in three different roles. The following details are common to all:
Engines 2 x 1600shp Rolls Royce Gnome H 1400—1 free power turbines.
Rotor Diameter 62′ 0″ **Length** 54′9″ **Height** 17′2″ **Max Weight** 23,500lb **Max Speed** 120 knots.
The 3 versions are:-

● RNAS CULDROSE　　　　　　　　　　　　　　　　**Sea King AEW**

AEW 2

Role: Airborne Early Warning. **Crew**: 1 pilot and 2 observers.
Avionics: Thorn/EMI searchwater radar. Marconi Orange Crop passive ESM equipment.
Armament: Nil.
Squadron Service: 849 HQ, 849A and 849B flights in commission.
Notes: Used to detect low flying aircraft trying to attack aircraft carrier battle groups under shipborne radar cover. Can also be used for surface search utilising its sophisticated, computerised long range radar. During 1987 849A flight will be embarked in HMS ILLUSTRIOUS and 849B in HMS ARK ROYAL. 849HQ acts as a training and trials unit at RNAS CULDROSE.

AUTHOR'S PHOTOGRAPH　　　　　　　　　　　　　**Sea King Mark IV**

HAS 5

Roles: Anti-submarine search and strike. SAR Transport.

Crew: 2 pilots, 1 observer and 1 aircrewman.

Avionics: MEL Sea Searcher radar; Plessey Type 195 variable depth active/passive sonar. GEC LAPADS passive sonobuoy analyses. Marconi Orange Crop passive ESM equipment.

Armament: 4 fuselage hardpoints capable of carrying STINGRAY, Mk 46/Mk 44 torpedoes or depth charges. Various flares, markers, grenades and sonobuoys can be carried internally and hand launched. A 7.62mm machine gun can be mounted in the doorway.

Squadron Service: 706, 810, 814, 819, 820, 824 and 826 squadrons in commission.

Notes: The SeaKing has been the backbone of the Fleet Air Arm's anti-submarine force since 1970. A further improved version, the HAS 6 is undergoing development. 706 is the advanced training squadron at RNAS CULDROSE. 810 is an operational training squadron with the capability to embark to reinforce the front line. During 1987, 814 squadron will be embarked in HMS ILLUSTRIOUS and 820 in HMS ARK ROYAL. 819 is shore based at PRESTWICK. 824 is a trials unit based at RNAS CULDROSE and 826 provides flights for service in RFA ships. The HAS 5 has a notable SAR capability which is frequently demonstrated in the south west approaches.

HMS GANNET

Sea King Mark V

HC 4

Role: Commando assault and utility transport.

Avionics: —

Crew: 1 pilot and 1 aircrewman.

Armament: Door mounted 7.62mm machine gun.

Squadron Service: 707, 845 and 846 squadrons in commission.

Notes: Capable of carrying up to 27 troops in the cabin or a wide variety of underslung loads up to 8,000lb in weight. 707 squadron is a training unit at RNAS YEOVILTON. 845 and 846 squadrons are based at YEOVILTON but able to embark or detach at short notice to support 3 Commando Brigade. The Sea King HC4 has a fixed undercarriage with no sponsons and no radome.

107

● S. KENT

Lynx

Westland LYNX

Variants: HAS 2, HAS 3
Roles: Surface search and strike; anti-submarine strike; SAR.
Engines: 2 x 900hp Rolls Royce GEM BS 360-07-26 free shaft turbines.
Rotor diameter: 42′0″ **Length** 39′1¼″ **Height** 11′ 0″ **Max Weight** 9,500lb.
Max Speed: 150 knots. **Crew**: 1 pilot and 1 observer.
Avionics: Ferranti SEA SPRAY radar. Marconi Orange Crop passive ESM equipment.
Armament: External pylons carry up to 4 x SEA SKUA air to surface missiles or 2 x STINGRAY, Mk 46 or Mk 44 torpedoes, depth charges, flares or markers.
Squadron Service: 702, 815 and 829 squadrons in commission.
Notes: 702 is a training squadron based at RNAS PORTLAND. 815, also based at Portland is the parent unit for single aircraft flights that embark in Type 42 destroyers and some classes of frigate, specialising in the surface strike role. 829 squadron parents flights in the Type 22 and other anti-submarine frigates.

Westland WASP HAS 1

● HMS OSPREY

Engine: 1 x 710shp Rolls Royce NIMBUS 103 free power turbine.
Crew: 1 pilot, 1 aircrewman and up to 3 passengers.
Notes: For years the Wasp was the standard helicopter carried by small ships. A few remain at sea parented by 829 squadron at RNAS PORTLAND but its replacement by the Lynx is almost complete and it is to be withdrawn from service during 1987.

Westland GAZELLE HT2

● P. HOLDGATE

Engine: 1 x 592shp Turbomeca ASTAZOU free power turbine.
Crew: 1 or 2 pilots.
Notes: In service with 705 squadron at RNAS CULDROSE. Used for training all RN helicopter pilots up to "wings standard" before they move onto the SeaKing or Lynx.

OTHER AIRCRAFT TYPES IN ROYAL NAVY SERVICE DURING 1987/88

● RNAS CULDROSE   **Jetstream**

British Aerospace JETSTREAM T2 and T3
Engines: 2 x 940hp Turbomeca ASTAZOU 16D turboprops. (T3 Garrett turboprops).
Crew: 1 or 2 pilots, 2 student observers plus 3 other seats.
Notes: A number of these aircraft are used by 750 squadron at RNAS CULDROSE for training Fleet Air Arm Observers.

de Havilland CHIPMUNK
Engine: 1 x 145hp de Havilland Gipsy Major 8 piston engine.
Crew: 2 pilots.
Notes: Used by the RN Flying Grading Flight at Roborough airport near Plymouth (and as such the first aircraft flown by generations of naval aircrew) and by stations flights at RNAS CULDROSE and YEOVILTON.

de Havilland SEA DEVON
Engines: 2 x 340hp de Havilland Gipsy Queen 70 piston engines.
Crew: 1 pilot, 1 aircrewman and up to 8 passengers.
Notes: 2 of these veteran transport aircraft remain as part of 771 squadron at RNAS CULDROSE.

de Havilland SEA HERON

Engines: 4 x 250hp de Havilland Gipsy Queen 30 piston engines.
Crew: 1 pilot, 1 aircrewman and up to 12 passengers.
Notes: In service since 1961, 4 of these excellent work horses remain in the station flight at RNAS YEOVILTON. They provide an inter-air station clipper service and support front line units with stores and transport.

British Aerospace CANBERRA TT18

Engines: 2 x 6500lb thrust Rolls Royce AVON turbojets.
Crew: 1 pilot and 1 observer.
Notes: Used by the (civilian manned) Fleet Requirements and Aircraft Direction Unit (FRADU) at RNAS YEOVILTON. Canberras provide towed targets for live firings by ships at sea.

Hawker HUNTER T8 and GA11

Engine: 1 x 7575lb thrust Rolls Royce AVON turbojet.
Crew: T8 1 or 2 pilots. GA11 1 pilot.
Notes: The Royal Navy has used Hunters to train fixed wing pilots since 1958. A number remain in service at RNAS YEOVILTON with the RN flying standards flight and with FRADU who use them as airborne targets for the aircraft direction school.

Westland WESSEX HU5

Engines: 2 x Rolls Royce GNOME free power turbines.
Crew: 1 or 2 pilots, 1 aircrewman and up to 12 passengers.
Notes: Now replaced in the commando assault role by the Seaking HC4. Wessex remain in small numbers with 771 Squadron at RNAS CULDROSE and 772 at RNAS PORTLAND, both on second line duties. All are due to be withdrawn from service by mid 1987.

In addition to these aircraft, the following aircraft have naval functions:
CANBERRA T17: Used by 360 joint RN/RAF squadron for electronic warfare tasks. Based at RAF WYTON.
British Aerospace 125: Two aircraft, owned by the RN are operated by RN aircrew as part of 32 squadron RAF based at RAF NORTHOLT.
The Fleet Air Arm Historic flight based at RNAS YEOVILTON has a **SWORDFISH, SEAHAWK, SEAFURY, FIREFLY and TIGER MOTH** on strength and these are often seen at air displays in the summer months.

Full details of these and many other naval aircraft can be found in AIRCRAFT OF THE ROYAL NAVY SINCE 1945.

At the end of the line . . .

Readers may well find other warships afloat which are not mentioned in this book. The majority have fulfilled a long and useful life and are now relegated to non-seagoing duties. The following list gives details of their current duties:

Penn. No.	Ship	Remarks
A134	RAME HEAD	Maintenance Ship. Used as an Accommodation Ship at Rosyth
A191	BERRY HEAD	As above, but at Devonport.
C35	BELFAST	World War II Cruiser Museum ship—Pool of London (Open to the public)
D73	CAVALIER	World War II Destroyer. Museum Ship at Brighton. (Open to the public).
D12	KENT	County Class Destroyer—Sea Cadet Training Ship at Portsmouth
F108 F113	LONDONDERRY FALMOUTH	Type 12 Frigates Harbour Training Ships—Gosport
F114	AJAX *B.o.*	Attached HMS RALEIGH as Static Training Ship
S05	FINWHALE	Porpoise Class Submarine Harbour Training Ship at Gosport
S67	ALLIANCE	Submarine Museum Ship at Gosport (Open to the public)

At the time of publishing the following ships were awaiting tow for scrap or sale.

PORTSMOUTH	MILFORD HAVEN	ROSYTH	
Nubian	Lewiston	Dreadnought	Shavington
Torquay	Eskimo	Lofoten	Crichton
Aveley	Woodlark	Crofton	Stalker
Ashanti	(Targets)	Yarmouth	Pollington
Alfriston			
Bickington			
Hodgeston			